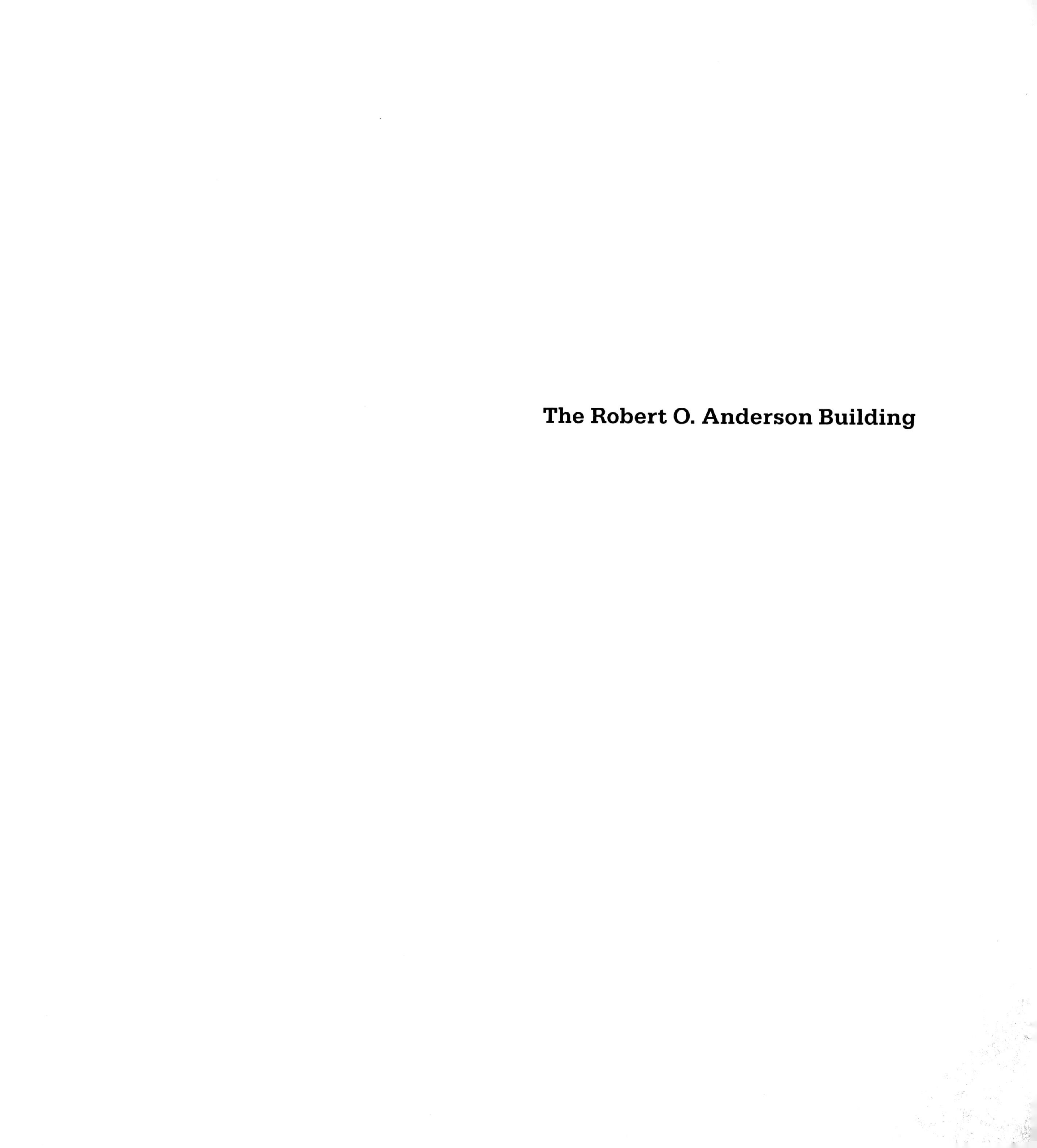

The Robert O. Anderson Building

The Robert O. Anderson Building

Los Angeles County Museum of Art

Photographs and illustrations

Pages 2–3, 5, 8, 10–11, 38, 42, 45 (bottom), 64–70: Peter Brenner, Photographic Services Department, Los Angeles County Museum of Art; pages 9, 12–16: Hardy Holzman Pfeiffer Associates; page 20 (bottom): Library of the Getty Center for the History of Art and the Humanities, Santa Monica; pages 21, 28, 30, 72–91: Photographic Services Department, Los Angeles County Museum of Art; page 24 (top): Gutekunst, Pennsylvania Academy of the Fine Arts, Philadelphia; page 24 (bottom): Pennsylvania Academy of the Fine Arts, Philadelphia; page 25: Harris/Davis Photo, Pennsylvania Academy of the Fine Arts Archives, Philadelphia; page 26 (top): © Art Institute of Chicago; pages 26 (bottom), 41 (right): Robert Winter; pages 32 (left), 33 (top): Robert E. Mates; pages 32 (right), 33 (bottom), 34 (top): Ezra Stoller, © ESTO; page 34 (bottom): Paschall/Taylor; page 35: Linda Lorenz; pages 40, 41 (left): Norman McGrath, courtesy Hardy Holzman Pfeiffer Associates; pages 44, 46 (top): courtesy Hardy Holzman Pfeiffer Associates; pages 45 (top), 46 (bottom): Cervin Robinson, courtesy Hardy Holzman Pfeiffer Associates.

Published by the Los Angeles County Museum of Art
5905 Wilshire Boulevard
Los Angeles, California 90036

Editor: Mitch Tuchman
Designer: Sandy Bell
Assistant designer: Robin Weiss
Production manager: Ann Isolde
Cover photograph: Peter Brenner

Type set in Primer and Serifa faces by Andresen Typographics, Los Angeles and Tucson.
Printed on Productolith Dull Book by Lithographix, Inc., Los Angeles. Cover printed on King James Cover; cover wrap, on Kimdura Translucent.

Library of Congress Cataloging in Publication Data
The Robert O. Anderson Building.
1. Robert O. Anderson Building (Los Angeles, Calif.) 2. Hardy Holzman Pfeiffer Associates.
3. Los Angeles (Calif.)—Buildings, structures, etc.
4. Art, Modern—20th century. 5. Los Angeles County
Museum of Art. I. Los Angeles County Museum of Art.
N582.L7R6 1986 727′.7′0922 86–20862

ISBN 0–87587–132–1

Contents

7 A Master Plan for a New Museum
Earl A. Powell III

19 Collection and Display: The Social History of Museum Space
Robert Winter

39 Hardy Holzman Pfeiffer Associates
Robert Winter

49 Construction Documentation
Photographs by Tim Street-Porter

64 Project Data: Construction and Materials

71 Selected Works from the Twentieth-Century Art Collection
Stephanie Barron

A Master Plan for a New Museum

Earl A. Powell III
Director

Rarely has an art museum been provided with an opportunity to withdraw for a moment in time to contemplate its future in the way that the Los Angeles County Museum of Art has in recent years. The building and expansion program that has been under way at the museum is one of the most far-reaching and comprehensive architectural developments among American cultural institutions. It concerns itself with the presentation of art and art collections in a way that newly represents the richness of what had been an assemblage of distinguished works of art and is now a more formally organized historical presentation of our visual heritage.

The opening of the Robert O. Anderson Building, a 115,000-square-foot structure comprising three levels of public gallery space and one of administrative and support space, concludes the first phase of the museum's master plan for development and construction. It culminates a planning and construction period that has involved the museum's Board of Trustees and staff since 1980, the year that planning began for a 35,000-square-foot addition to the Ahmanson Building.

Coincident with the planning for the Ahmanson addition, the Board of Trustees requested that I initiate, along with its Facilities Committee, a search for an architectural firm to undertake a new building for modern and contemporary art. This was conceived as a 30,000-square-foot building, hardly more than a quarter the size of the eventual Anderson edifice, for which the Atlantic Richfield Company proposed a generous lead gift. That gift in turn impelled the museum to rethink its entire collections and architectural program.

In the next six months I traveled throughout the United States with staff and various trustees looking at new architecture and interviewing firms we believed would be appropriate for the museum's project. In 1981, after numerous exhaustive interviews, the architectural firm of Hardy Holzman Pfeiffer Associates (HHPA) was selected to develop a master plan that would address the museum's historical evolution over the past twenty years and anticipate its needs for new galleries and support space, including the Anderson Building. HHPA was selected not only on the basis of its presentation to the trustees but also on the basis of its impressive credits. HHPA had long been active in museum renovation and construction and other cultural planning and design projects. They had reorganized the St. Louis Museum brilliantly and had undertaken major projects at the Cooper-Hewitt Museum in New York City, the Toledo Museum, and the Virginia Museum of Fine Arts. In each of these cases they had united new architectural design with older buildings.

Their effort at the Los Angeles County Museum of Art would be their largest museum project to date and the most complicated. In less than twenty years the original gallery complex had simply been overwhelmed. What we needed was not only a new building added to the original three but, even more important, a reorganization of collections that had not been available to the public.

The Los Angeles County Museum of Art as a general cultural institution displays in permanent installations and changing exhibitions art of both Eastern and Western hemispheres and both ancient and modern times. It was with a great sense of excitement and anticipation, therefore, that the staff began to work with the architects on the development of a master plan that would involve the reorganization of collections and the reallocation of space. The new building for twentieth-century art thus became less an end in itself than the culmination of a planning and design program that addressed the needs of every aspect of the museum: its collections and their conservation and our administrative organization. This process was one of the most far-reaching in the American museum world in recent years, and as such it is worth recounting.

During 1981 the museum's curatorial staff met frequently with the architectural staff of HHPA to develop new gallery plans for their collections. Using the construction of the William Pereira-designed Ahmanson addition as a major incentive, new gallery configura-

Ground breaking for the Robert O. Anderson Building January 9, 1984.

The Ahmanson *enfilade:* from the seventeenth-century Dutch and Flemish painting gallery through the eighteenth-century European painting and sculpture gallery into the nineteenth-century European painting and sculpture gallery.

tions were designed. These were implemented as part of the early construction program in order to begin to realize the new presentation, chronologically and historically, of the museum's collections. The Ahmanson addition, making valuable space available for the museum's European galleries and for its decorative arts and American collections, opened in 1983 to great critical and scholarly acclaim as the initial direction of our building and installation program was unveiled to the public.

The relocated collections in the original Ahmanson Building and its addition also involved the greatly expanded reinstallation of our pre-Columbian collection, augmented by the magnificent promised gift of Constance McCormick Fearing. This made a very elegant presentation of pre-Columbian art possible. Our American collections were also installed in renovated galleries. Decorative arts were given additional space and greater prominence in the new program in order to highlight the great collection of monumental silver donated by Mr. and Mrs. Arthur Gilbert along with their extraordinary and unique collection of mosaics. The Gilbert galleries on the Plaza level of the Ahmanson Building are the focal point of our decorative arts collections.

On the second level of the Ahmanson Building the European collections of painting, sculpture, and decorative arts were installed in order to allow a visitor to proceed sequentially from medieval art in the existing building through late nineteenth-century art in skylighted galleries in the new Ahmanson addition, then to the gallery bridge connecting the addition to the second level of the Frances and Armand Hammer Building. Temporary new galleries for prints and drawings and for photography and a presentation space for our exhibition program in twentieth-century art were placed on the second level as well.

With the opening of the Anderson Building these programs move once more: prints and drawings along with photography into new galleries in the refurbished second level of the Hammer Building, and twentieth-century art, of course, into the two floors of permanent

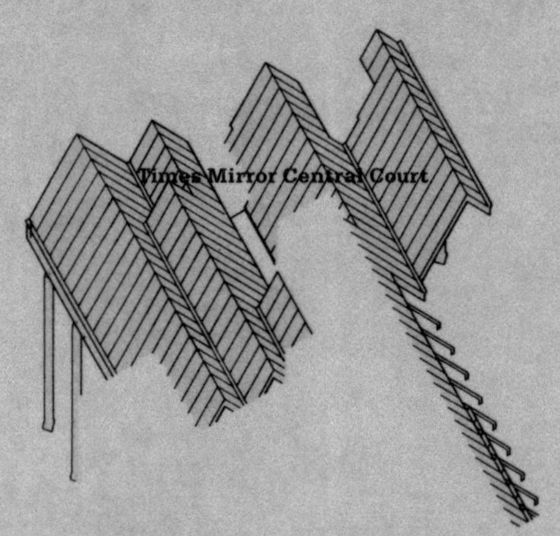
Times Mirror Central Court

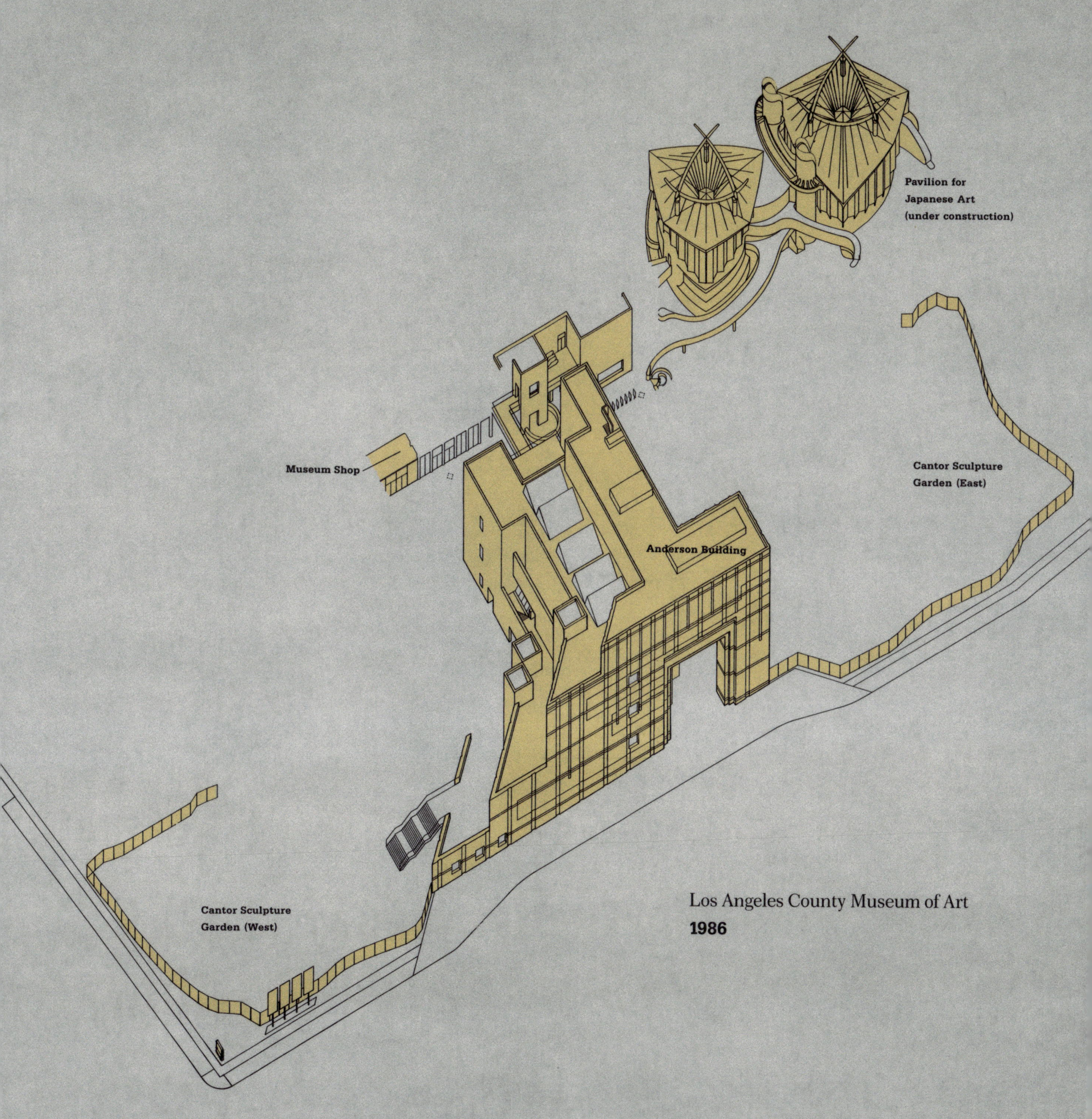

Los Angeles County Museum of Art

1986

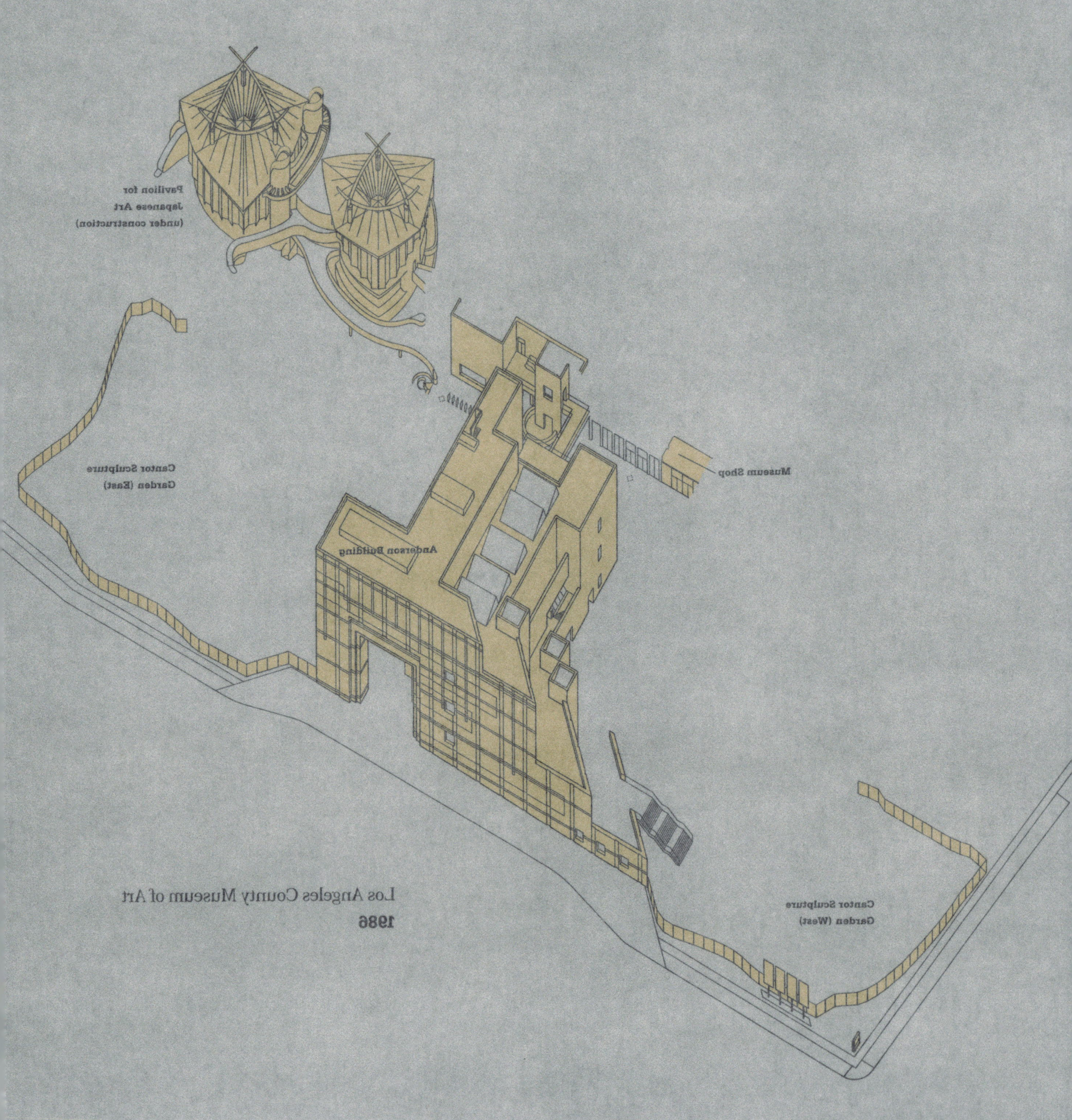

Pavilion for
Japanese Art
(under construction)
Cantor Sculpture
Garden (East)
Museum Shop
Anderson Building
Los Angeles County Museum of Art
1986
Cantor Sculpture
Garden (West)

Los Angeles County Museum of Art

1983

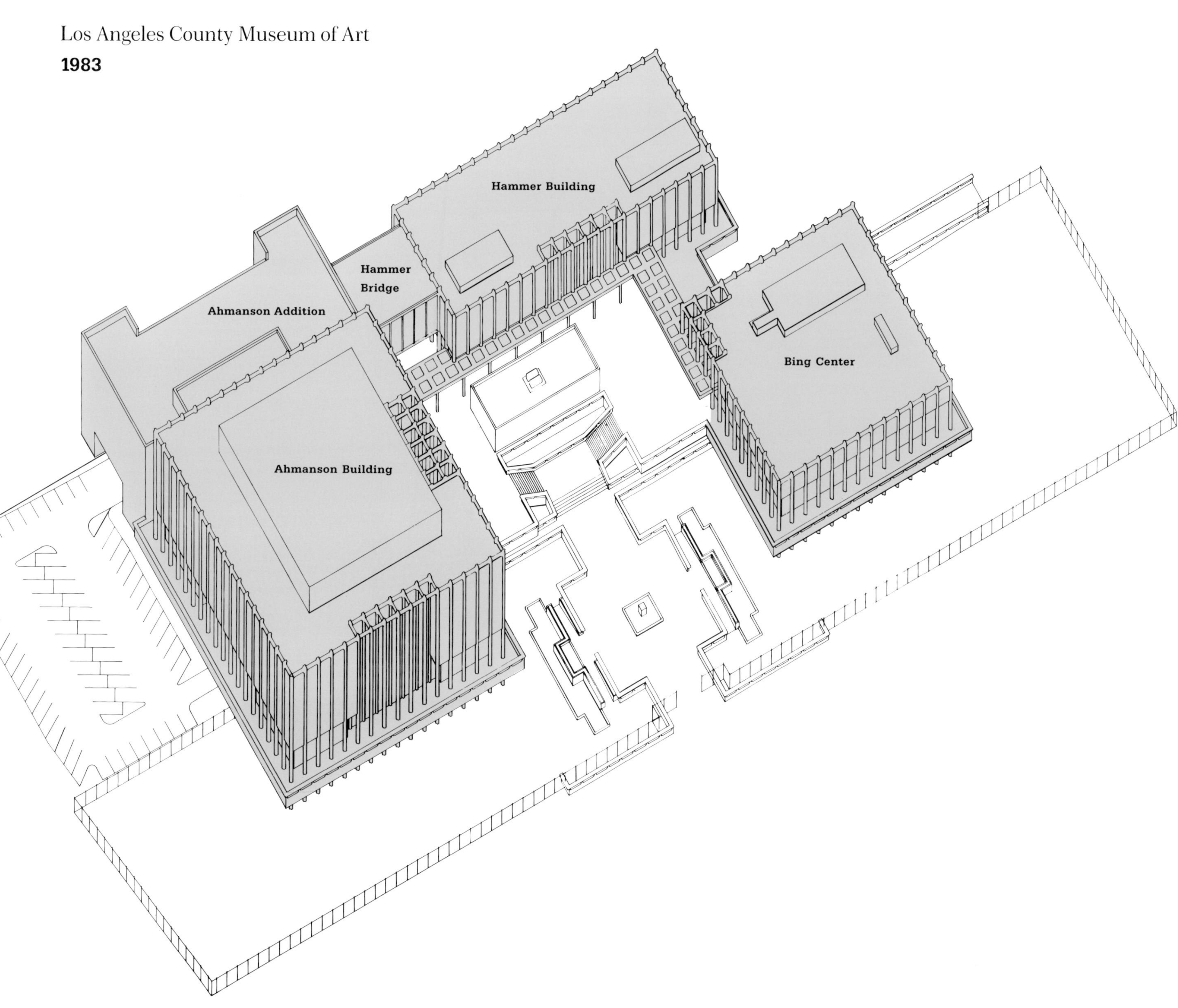

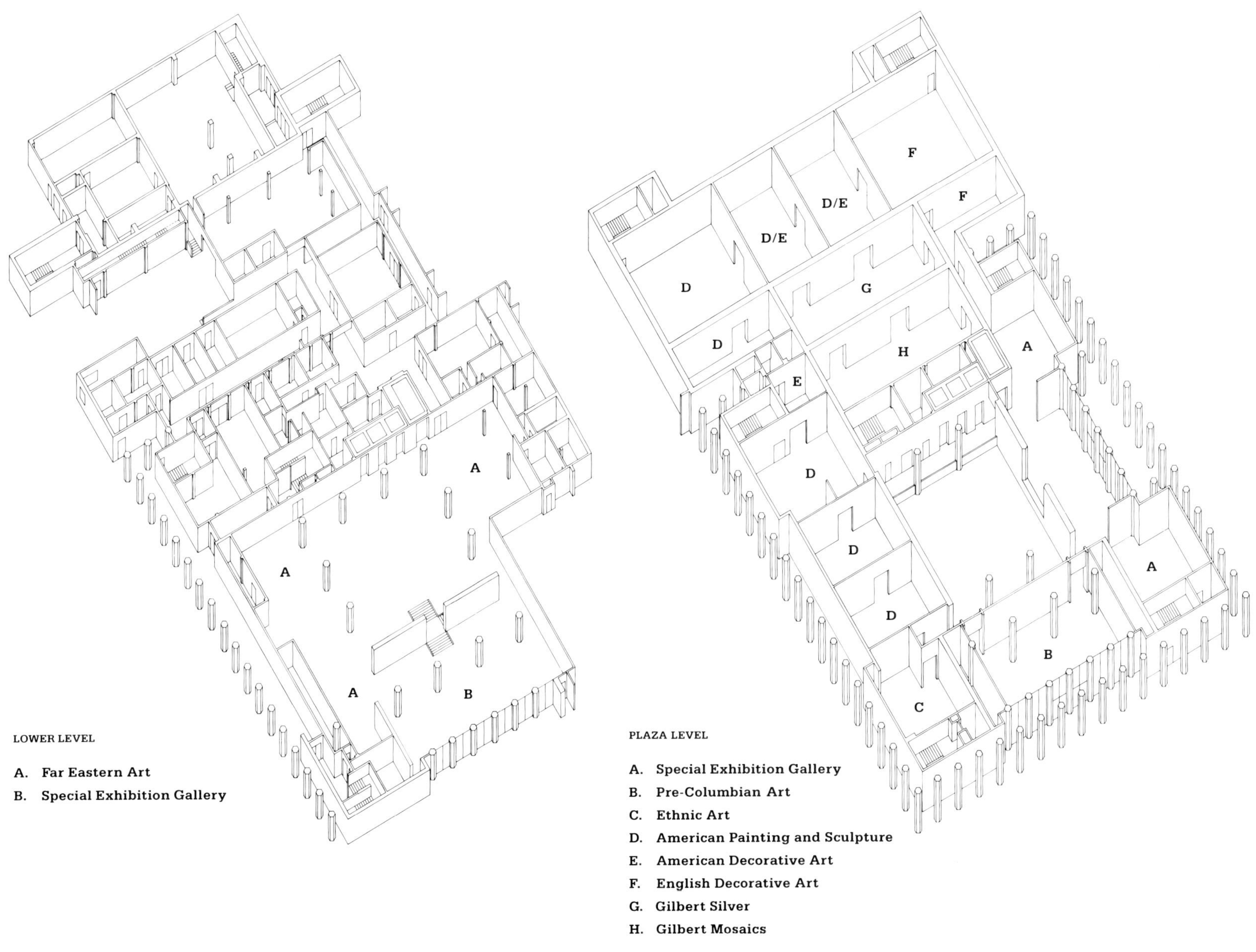

The Ahmanson Building

collection galleries in the Anderson Building itself. In the space thus vacated on the second level of the Ahmanson Building, we will finally install our distinguished collection of ancient art, allowing a visitor to the museum to begin to experience the art of the Western hemisphere in the Greco-Roman galleries on the east side of the Ahmanson, proceeding around the building and its addition, across the bridge, through the Hammer, and into the Anderson and its galleries for twentieth-century art.

On the third floor of the Ahmanson Building are the Indian collections, the most distinguished in the United States, which have been given a new installation along with our Islamic collection. The Doris Stein Research and Design Center for Costumes and Textiles, another major new development, is also on the third floor. The center, dedicated in May 1986, includes a new library and storage facilities that permit the collection to be housed in a manner conducive to accessibility, conservation, and scholarship.

Clearly the museum's master plan has

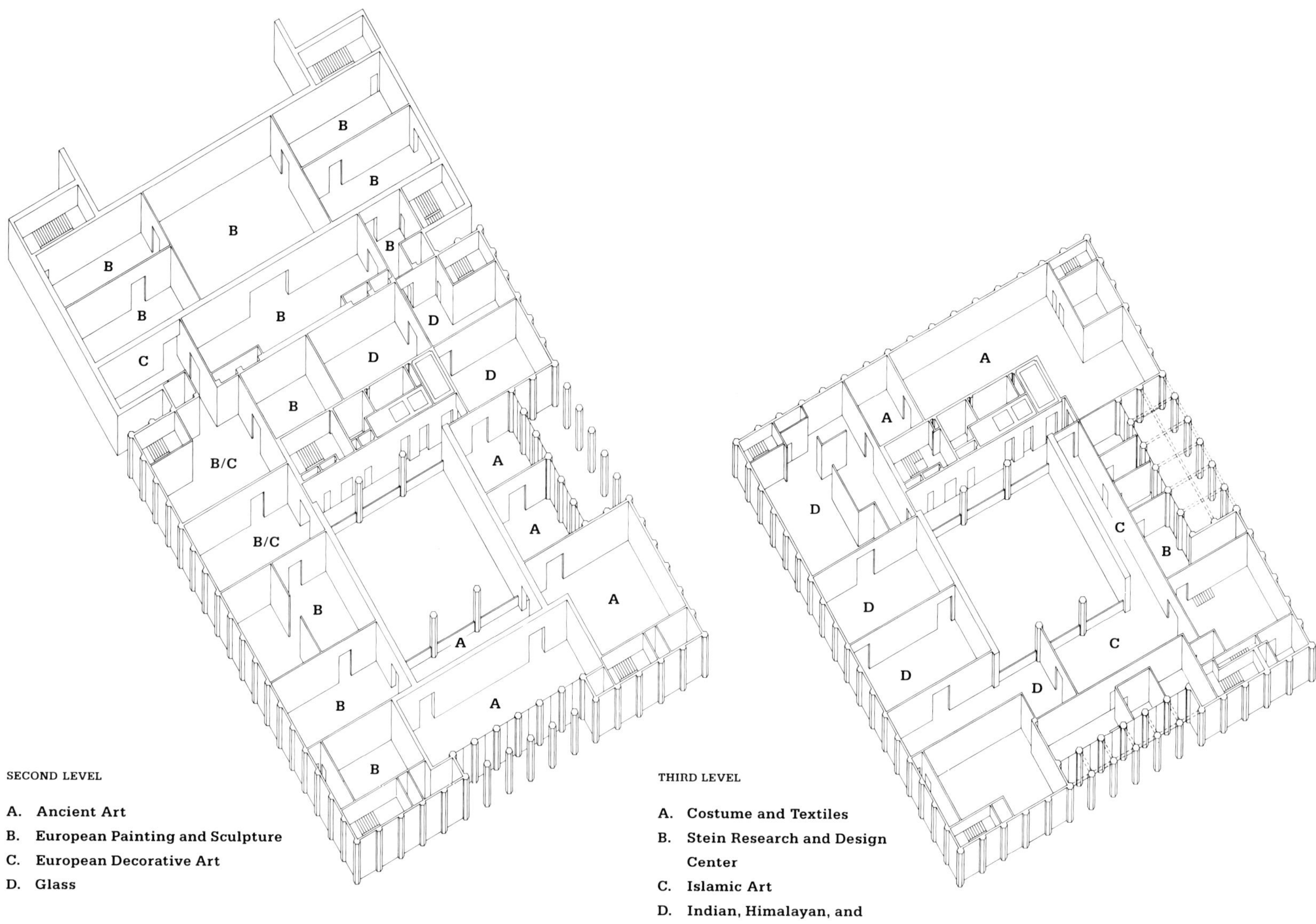

SECOND LEVEL

A. Ancient Art
B. European Painting and Sculpture
C. European Decorative Art
D. Glass

THIRD LEVEL

A. Costume and Textiles
B. Stein Research and Design Center
C. Islamic Art
D. Indian, Himalayan, and Southeast Asian Art

added much-needed space. Even more important, that space evolved from a dedicated curatorial staff and a sensitive and creative architectural firm's collaborating to present the public with a new experience of the Los Angeles County Museum of Art's collection. I think in many ways the reinstallation of the collections in the Ahmanson Building has been as important to the presentation of the collections as the new architecture of the Anderson Building will be for twentieth-century art.

Sometimes the most difficult problems are overcome by the simplest solutions. The underlying rationale for the development of the new gallery installations in our architectural program was based on a new visitor circulation pattern that simplifies the rather complex one that had evolved over twenty years of changing use and growth within the museum. At the ground level, particularly with the construction of the Conservation Center in the Hammer Building, an entirely new administrative organization has evolved, which has rationalized the space. New offices are located in the Anderson Building, and for the first time the majority of our curatorial and administrative staff will be located in a common office complex.

The decision to locate the Anderson Building on Wilshire Boulevard may seem an obvious one, but the museum studied various options before concluding with the architects that the Wilshire location was best. The location of the building at the front of the museum complex gives us a dynamic new presence in the rapidly growing Wilshire Boulevard area as well as a new front door. It is also obvious that the architects related the facade of the new building to details of the existing architecture. The large new entrance has exactly the same proportions as the major opening on the Ahmanson facade, and the columns of the original buildings are replicated in the vertical articulation of the Anderson facade.

The entrance stairway leads to the Times Mirror Central Court. This three-story 40,000-square-foot area is designed to serve as the architectural, visual, and symbolic focus for the entire museum complex. The partially roofed Central Court covers nearly an acre and is bounded by the museum's four buildings: the Ahmanson Building to the west, the Hammer

The Anderson Building

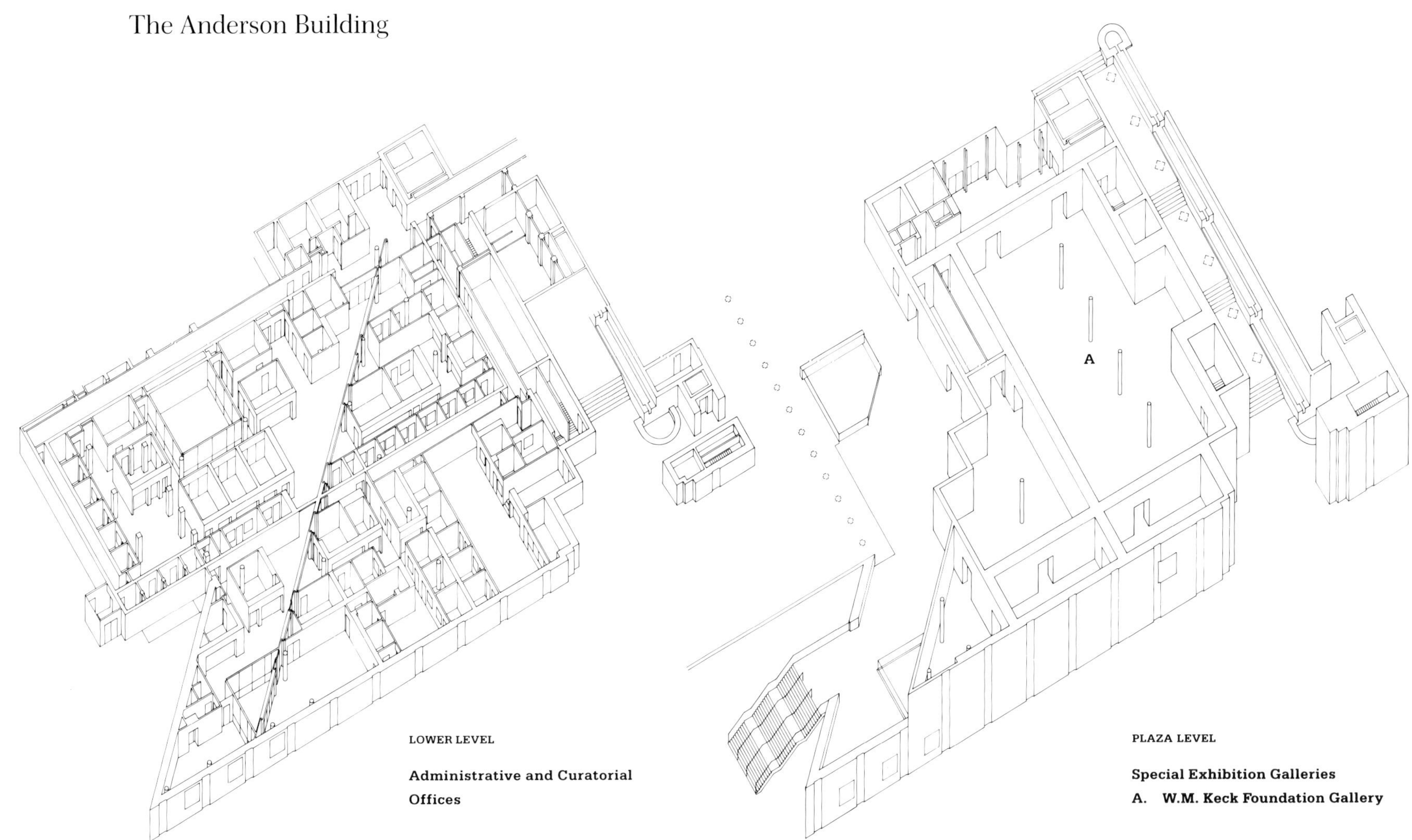

LOWER LEVEL

Administrative and Curatorial Offices

PLAZA LEVEL

Special Exhibition Galleries
A. W.M. Keck Foundation Gallery

Building to the north, the Bing Center to the east, and the Anderson Building to the south. The Central Court includes a new admissions and information kiosk as well as the Museum Shop, newly relocated under the Hammer Bridge and expanded to 3,500 feet.

The Robert O. Anderson Building provides more than 50,000 square feet of exhibition galleries for the twentieth-century collections and for special exhibitions. The gallery design is based on the Beaux-Arts concept of the *enfilade*, a sequence of galleries offering clear directional vistas. Separate entrances off the Times Mirror Central Court will make it possible to present exhibitions of different aspects of twentieth-century art simultaneously or to open the entire level for a single major presentation in the new Plaza level galleries, including the grand W.M. Keck Foundation Gallery.

The Plaza level sculpture court, donated by Mr. and Mrs. B. Gerald Cantor, very sensitively relates the Anderson and Ahmanson buildings to each other and creates the effect of an outdoor gallery between them. On the second level the sculpture plaza donated by Mr. and Mrs. Bram Goldsmith offers an outdoor exhibition area for the display of contemporary sculpture.

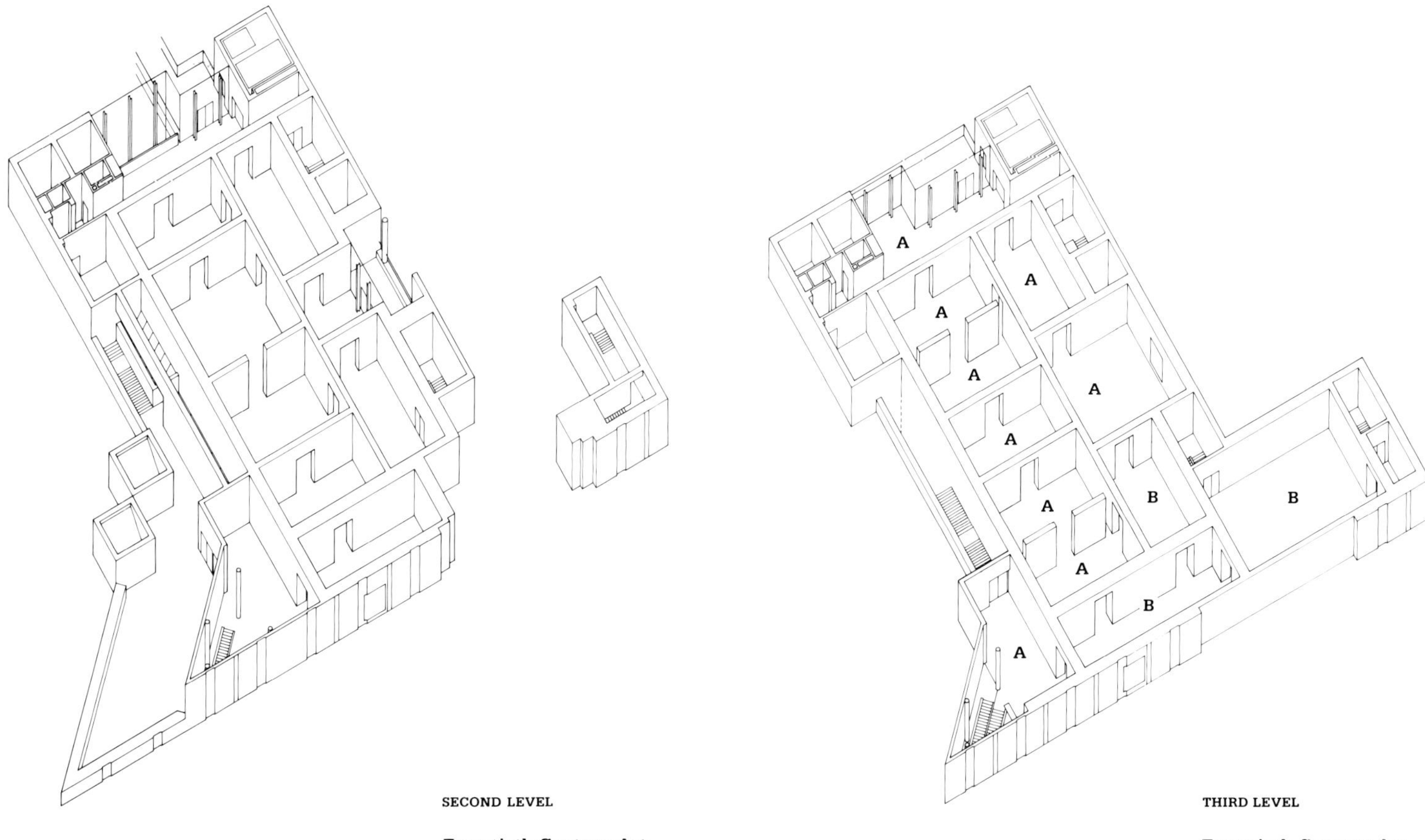

SECOND LEVEL

Twentieth-Century Art
American Art since 1960

THIRD LEVEL

Twentieth-Century Art
A. European Art 1900–1950
B. Abstract Expressionism

The Hammer Building

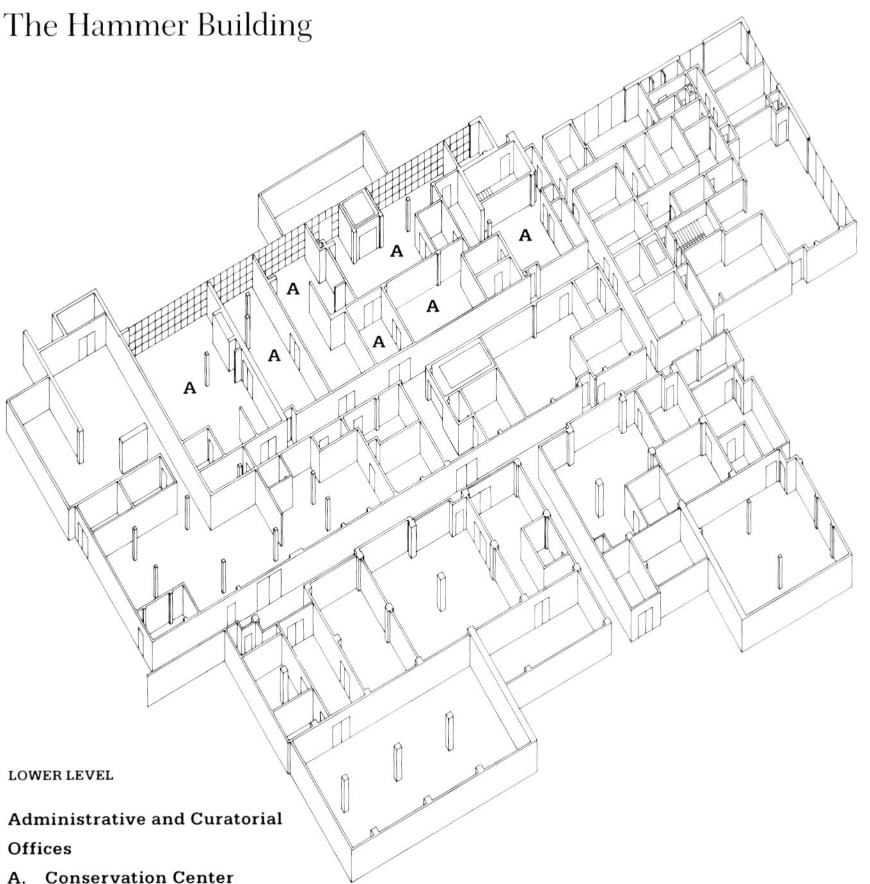

LOWER LEVEL

Administrative and Curatorial Offices
A. Conservation Center

The master plan also calls for the development of new sculpture installations in the east and west B. Gerald Cantor Sculpture Gardens, a new center for education, a new library with compact shelving, and the Dorothy Collins Brown Auditorium. The Robert Gore Rifkind Center for German Expressionist Studies, now under construction, will open in early 1987. A year later the Pavilion for Japanese Art, a fascinating new structure specifically designed for the display of the screens and scrolls of the Shin'enkan Collection, will open. Additional plans call for the spanning of the present Ahmanson Building atrium along with new installations of the B. G. Cantor gifts, the museum's distinguished David Daniels Collection of medals, and our fine collection of ancient art. Thus while the completion of the Robert O. Anderson Building represents the conclusion of one phase of major construction and reorganization at the museum, it does not conclude our development program. As the museum approaches its twenty-fifth anniversary, it will continue to evolve and grow, keeping pace with its rapidly growing collections.

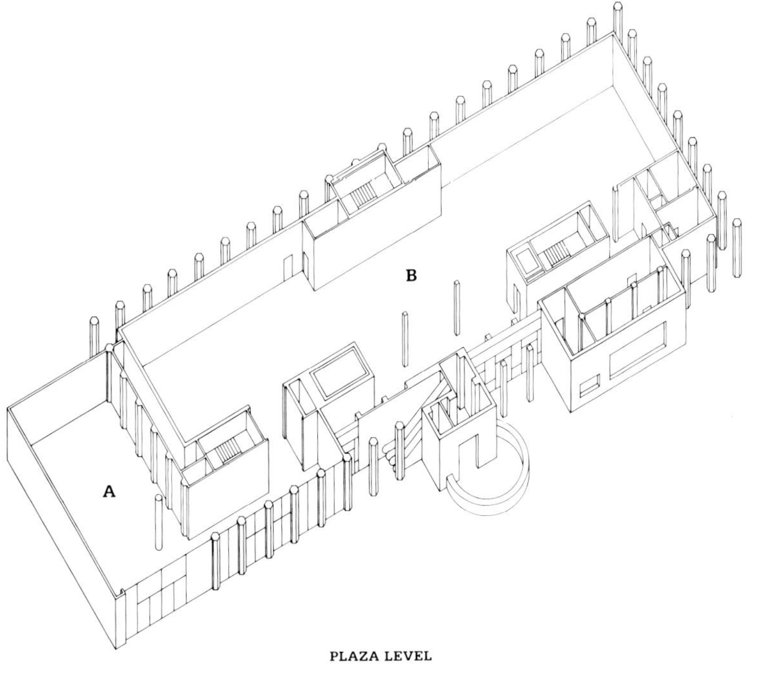

PLAZA LEVEL

A. Museum Shop
B. Special Exhibition Gallery

SECOND LEVEL

A. Hammer Collection
B. Prints and Drawings
C. Photography

The Bing Center

LOWER LEVEL

A. Rifkind Study Center (opens 1987)
B. Art Research Library
C. Education Department
D. Art Rental Gallery

PLAZA LEVEL

A. Bing Theater Ticket Desk
B. Plaza Cafe
C. Bing Theater

SECOND LEVEL

A. Bing Theater

18

But in all respects our age is obsessed with wanting to show things only in their natural surroundings, and thereby with suppressing the essential event, the mental act which isolates things from reality. Nowadays a painting is "presented" amidst furniture, knick-knacks, hangings of the same period—a dull decor composed by the lady of the house, who, once ignorant, has spent her days in archives and libraries. In the middle of all this display the masterpiece we view while dining doesn't give us the same intoxicating joy we should expect only in a museum, which symbolizes all the more by its austerity the interior spaces into which the artist withdrew in order to create.

—Marcel Proust, *Remembrance of Things Past*
(translation: Susan Grayson)

Collection and Display
The Social History of Museum Space

Robert Winter

Surveying a national phenomenon of museum construction in the 1960s and early 1970s, the distinguished architectural critic Paul Goldberger believed that the great wave of museum building had subsided.[1] Nevertheless, planning and construction went right on so that today there is hardly an art museum in America that is not engaged in a major building program or at least looking forward to one. Many of the world's best architects are involved and getting prizes for their designs. A spate of newspaper articles has called attention recently to the phenomenon.[2]

Obviously this activity is spurred by the great popular interest in art. The museums have been successful in drawing people to them, often with blockbuster exhibitions such as *Treasures of Tutankhamun* and *A Day in the Country*. New museums are needed as the country experiences demographic shifts to cities like Fort Lauderdale and San Jose. A great deal of art, furthermore, is coming out of private collections and going public, so to speak. And surely more art is being produced today than at any other time in the history of the human race.

In this proliferation we see also the glorification of museums as symbols of civic pride. It is happening all over the country where museums have even been used as vehicles of urban coming of age. The Portland (Maine) Museum building was a conscious and successful ploy in that city's urban renewal program. And while the Robert O. Anderson Building was placed on Wilshire Boulevard primarily as the result of functional considerations, it is no coincidence that it literally transforms the approach along the great commercial artery of our city. Its vast, welcoming gate salutes the fact that art and Los Angeles have made it—big!

The architects of the new museums are being challenged, moreover, by intangibles of the future. Their buildings must be adaptable to the changing concepts of what art is. Architects must employ the very latest mechanical devices that pertain to the display of art and somehow leave room for future inventions. They must provide space for expressions as yet undreamed of. As if these considerations were not enough, they must somehow incorporate the social customs of their time and yet realize that these also change.

Needless to say, these increased expectations of what a museum should be broaden and make much more complex the role of the architect who must now take on the new duties of an impresario as well as the old ones of developing the best possible galleries in which to display works of art. The building itself must make an artistic statement, and yet architecture, the mother of the arts, must never repress her children. As any mother knows, this is no easy assignment.

Words, pictures, and floor plans can never really create the feeling of museum space and its relationship to the objects within it, but in the pages that follow I will try to suggest what museums should be, how architecture relates to art, and how conceptions about that relationship are changing. In this way we position the Robert O. Anderson Building and its architects, Hardy Holzman Pfeiffer Associates, on the museum scene.

Museums were born when people first stored possessions because they were thought to be holy or valuable or beautiful or all of these. In this way, as Theodor Adorno has written, the museum resembles a necropolis, populated as it is with things past.[3] Yet the museum is forever capable of inspiring delight, just as an orchestra does when it "revives" a Mozart symphony at each performance. The pharoahs of ancient Egypt advanced the acquisitive idea when they tried to take things with them into the afterlife. The Greeks settled for something less when they stored the booty of battle in temples, the Athenian Treasury (c. 485 B.C.) at Delphi being a famous example.

It was the Greeks who apparently built the first picture galleries; in the second century A.D. the Greek historian Pausanias described the pictures still hanging in the Pinacotheke (built after 404 B.C.), the little building that flanked the north side of the Propylaea on the

Fig. 1 Pinacotheke, Athens, Greece.

Acropolis at Athens (fig. 1). The exterior was dominated by a porch with three Doric columns. Pausanias did not describe the gallery itself, but what remains today is a rectangular room with one door opening onto the porch and two asymmetrically placed windows framed with pilasters that retain traces of polychromy. The paintings may have been hung from moldings or exhibited on easels.[4] That is all we know about the building and of the way that it functioned in Greek life.

We know nothing about the lighting in the Pinacotheke or the thought of the architect, Mnesicles, that went into its other amenities for viewing the paintings, but from knowing the way some other Greek buildings functioned, we suspect that the gallery would not be considered adequate by modern standards. We do not even know whether the Pinacotheke was a public place. With these sparse records our social history of museum space begins.

We know much more about the way art functioned in ancient Rome. Baths, temples, basilicas—all were decorated with sculpture and painting. Furthermore, as Sigfried Giedion pointed out in *Architecture and the Phenomena of Transition* (1971), Roman architects were the first to see architecture as space-containing rather than space-emanating.[5] Unlike the Egyptians and Greeks, who seemed more concerned with exterior space and who left their interiors with lines, sometimes forests, of columns dimly lit, the Romans concentrated on interior space, shaping architectural elements in order to create a dramatic, sometimes awesome effect. The Pantheon (fig. 2) is probably the most complete remaining realization of this conception, but a walk through the ruins of the Baths of Caracalla is enough to make clear the Roman discovery of the excitement of vast volumes of space broken by arches and columns. And it takes only a little more imagination to realize the splendor of their adornment with painting and sculpture.

The Roman patricians were, of course, passionate collectors especially of Greek works and copies thereof. "What do you suppose has come of the wealth of foreign nations who are

Fig. 2 Giovanni Battista Piranesi (Italy, 1720–78), *Interior View of the Pantheon*, engraved plate in *Vedute di Roma* (Views of Rome), undated.

now so poor," wrote Cicero about these collections in the first century B.C., "when you see Athens, Pergamum, Cyzicus, Miletus, Samos—nay, all Asia and Achaea, all Greece and Sicily, concentrated in these few houses?"[6] But again these collections were private and rarely seen by outsiders. There was little need for extensive museum space.

The patrons of art during the Middle Ages also screened their most precious possessions from public view. Cathedrals, of course, were open to the public and presumably were enjoyed by all classes, but what were then considered their greatest treasures were, at best, seen from afar (fig. 3). The wonders of *The Treasury of San Marco* at the museum in 1985 reminded us that the Middle Ages were not so dark as once supposed, but it should be remembered that the richly enameled and bejeweled artifacts that we saw (through an elaborate security system, to be sure) were usually not on display in medieval times; they were brought out of their safe places, if ever, only for feast days and special masses. The Renaissance, in spite of its reputation for producing and amassing the fine arts, was no less secretive about them. Art was aristocratic and far beyond the reach of the public. Museums were still private and elitist. The *grand galerie* at the Louvre was built in 1610 as a corridor connecting Louis XIII's main palace to the Tuileries and was soon filled with the royal accumulation of artworks. Although it was a private gallery, it inspired its few visitors as a model for museums that were to follow. The echoes of its high, skylighted hall, broken up into smaller galleries articulated by sets of columns, were to be heard in many a nineteenth-century art museum, although perhaps never again with such grandiose flair.

Mordaunt Crook in his study of the British Museum has noted the significance of the grand galerie as a last gesture of royalty about to be set aside by the democratic spirit. "In fact," he wrote, "the emergence of the modern museum seems at times almost an index of royal decline. Although architecturally trivial by comparison with [the Museum Fredericianum at] Cassel, the Charleston Museum in South Carolina, U.S.A., was perhaps a more significant portent: it was founded in 1773, the year of the Boston Tea Party."[7]

Such significant changes in Western society would soon open the doors of the princes and bishops. The first sign of the democratization of art was its secularization. The same impulse that inspired the scientist to separate animals into species and minerals into elements prompted the post-Renaissance connoisseur of art to look for styles and schools and to see relationships among them. Archaeology and art history were born, and as great collections were amassed, new space was needed. One can see the beginnings of this in the scientific revolution of the seventeenth century when the rich and well-born added collections of flora and fauna to their collections of painting, sculpture, and decorative arts in order both to

Fig. 3 Pieter Neefs the Elder (Flanders, c. 1578–1656/61), *Interior of the Antwerp Cathedral*, 1612, oil on panel, 24 x 31 in., William Randolph Hearst Collection, Los Angeles County Museum of Art.

Fig. 4 Charles Willson Peale (United States, 1741 – 1827), *The Artist in His Museum*, 1822, oil on canvas, 103 3/4 x 79 7/8 in., presented by Mr. R. Patterson, Joseph and Sarah Harrison Collection, Pennsylvania Academy of the Fine Arts.

Fig. 5 Facade, British Museum, London, England, about 1857.

satisfy curiosity and to enhance the amateur's adventure into science—thus a full cabinet of curiosities.[8] Such a gallery was arranged in Independence Hall by the early nineteenth-century American painter and naturalist Charles Willson Peale. His painting *The Artist in His Museum*, 1822 (fig. 4), shows him raising a curtain on an exhibition of paintings ranked high above cases of stuffed animals, behind him a mastodon bone that he had unearthed near Newburgh, New York, in a pioneering dig. Lest we find this kind of museum quaint, we should remember that the coupling of art history and natural history lasted well into the twentieth century. It was as late as 1964 that the Los Angeles County Museum of Art itself finally broke its physical ties with the Museum of Natural History and moved from Exposition to Hancock Park.

Some privileged commoners had, of course, been allowed to see private collections before the emergence of democracy in the eighteenth century. A few had even entered Philip II's hermetic Escorial outside Madrid. Their entrance, like the collections they viewed, however, reflected the royal whim. The didactic Enlightenment, by contrast, regarded the public museum as a means of spreading learning, an absolute necessity in the new age of the people. Even so, except in England, the popularly accessible museum was not to emerge until the very end of the eighteenth century. In France it took a revolution to open the Louvre.

An early effect of the rise of democratic ideas was the founding of the British Museum in 1753. At first it was not very democratic and was simply a repository of a natural history collection (later moved to South Kensington) and a large library of predominantly political books and documents. It was accommodated in Montagu House, a late seventeenth-century mansion in the Bloomsbury district of London.

In the early nineteenth century the British Museum began to acquire archaeological treasures largely as a result of British conquest and colonialism. Suddenly the natural history section was overwhelmed by antiquities, the greatest of which were the Elgin Marbles (acquired

1815), and it was seen that a new building was needed to exhibit them properly and to house a growing and much-diversified library. That is the reason for the great Ionic pile that we see today (fig. 5).

The history of that building, designed by Sir Robert Smirke (1823), is beautifully told by Mordaunt Crook.[9] Suffice it to say that the British Museum, the first great museum to be built for the edification of the public rather than for the fancy of the nobility, is significant for its development of exterior and interior space, becoming a model for museums throughout the English-speaking world. One enters through a magnificent Ionic porch into a fine, high foyer (fig. 6). To the left is a grand staircase, the *sine qua non* of future museum building. Straight ahead was, for a short time, an outdoor quadrangle, soon to be filled up by the present Round Reading Room. Around this central plan were distributed the galleries for the archaeological collection on the left and the library on the right.

This plan and the noble facade were not without precedent. We are reminded of the well-published project for a museum (1803) designed by the Frenchman J. N. L. Durand, which made the same use of a forest of columns, though it did not have the U-shape of Smirke's masterpiece. Four other classically porticoed museums were being built at the same time as the British Museum: the Glyptothek (1816–30) designed by Leo von Klenze in Munich, the even grander Altes Museum (1823–30) by Karl Freidrich Schinkel in Berlin, the City Art Gallery (1823) by Sir Charles Barry in Manchester, and the Royal Scottish Academy (1822–26) by W. H. Playfair in Edinburgh.[10]

The British Museum was representative rather than original, but as the repository of one of the most remarkable collections of ancient art, it became a reference point for museum architects. The concern shown for proper lighting, even though not completely successful there, became an obsession too. The relationship at the British Museum between art and architectural detail, often criticized by nineteenth-century experts as too strong for the proper exposition of the art (fig. 7), would be a central question hotly debated in the construction of new museums. Certainly the great columned front would be an inspiration for museologists for years to come: a museum "should be" Greco-Roman.

The facade and the arrangement of galleries exhibited in the floor plan sum up the progress of thinking about museums in the first third of the nineteenth century. Both would be affirmed by developments in the late nineteenth century. In the meantime, however, a stylistic phenomenon occurred that was more important for exterior space than for interior arrangements: in the mid- century the ideas of John Ruskin were published in his extremely popular *Seven Lamps of Architecture* (1848) and *The Stones of Venice* (1851). In many ways Ruskin's ideas are seminal to an understanding of the Victorian mind. In sum what he did was encourage a renewal of the Gothic Revival that had begun with late eighteenth-century romanticism. An even broader effect, however, was to advance the conception of architecture as an excursion into the most florid, not to say, frenzied, realms of the imagination.

Ruskin himself was directly associated with this interpretation of his words in the building of the Oxford Museum (1854–58), though he lived to regret that association.[11] Whatever his afterthoughts, it is a remarkable building, especially its huge train-shed central hall. But what is really notable is that Ruskin's extraordinary popularity came precisely at the time of North America's first major museum-building program. While the first museums in the United States were classically inclined, the large ones of the period just before the Civil War would not look like the British Museum at all, at least on the exterior.[12] Influenced by the rich prose of Ruskin, architects of museums would build pseudomedieval palaces for the arts and accepting the invitation to stray from classical sobriety, go even further in their creativity.

Even before the cult of Ruskin was formed, Ithiel Towne and Alexander Jackson Davis convinced the trustees of the Wadsworth Athe-

Fig. 6 **L. W. Collman (England, 1816–81), *Front Hall of the British Museum*, 1847, watercolor, 20 1/8 x 26 7/8 in., British Museum.**

Fig. 7 **Ethnology gallery, British Museum, London, England, about 1920.**

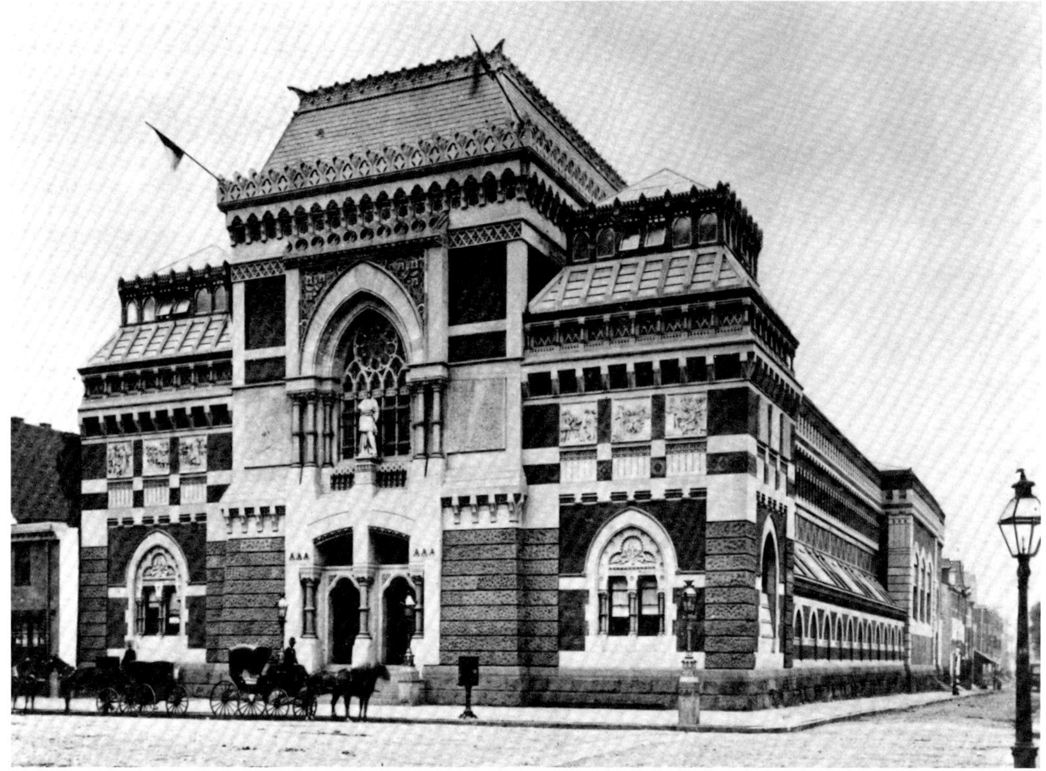

Fig. 8 Facade, Pennsylvania Academy of the Fine Arts, Philadelphia, 1876.

Fig. 10 Gallery F, 63rd Annual Exhibition, Pennsylvania Academy of the Fine Arts, Philadelphia, 1893.

neum at Hartford that they should erect a Gothic museum (1842). This was followed a few years later by the building of the Smithsonian Institution (1841–55), designed by James Renwick, Jr., in a hybrid of Romanesque and Gothic. For his next museum design Renwick showed a surprising knowledge of the latest thing in Paris by choosing the Neo-Mansart (mansard in Britain and North America) style of Louis Napoleon's additions to the Louvre for the Corcoran (now Renwick) Gallery (1859–74) in Washington, D.C. More clearly Ruskinian in derivation was Peter B. Wright's rendering for the National Academy of Design (1862) in New York and his Street Hall (1864–66) at Yale University, the former unfortunately demolished, the latter disfigured beyond recall.

But the greatest of these Ruskinian extravaganzas, beautifully restored for the bicentennial of the American revolution, was the Pennsylvania Academy of the Fine Arts (1872–76) in Philadelphia. Designed by Frank Furness and George W. Hewitt, it was probably the most flamboyant example of Victorian polychromy in North America when it was built, a weird interpretation of Venetian Gothic capped with a mansard roof (fig. 8). As with all great architecture, it must be experienced *in situ*—in this case to be believed.

The ground-floor entry is surprisingly plain and leads off into libraries, lecture rooms, and museum offices toward the rear, but the grand staircase immediately invites the visitor to the second level, where the hall is as dazzling as the facade. Gilded and painted walls open on three sides with wide Venetian Gothic arches that lead to the galleries. Everything seems to move, including the nervously wrought light standards on the newel posts (fig. 9).

After this display, the architecture of the restored galleries is somewhat disappointing, possibly because they too have been cleaned up. A few of Furness's mad details entertain the eye, but otherwise the rectangular spaces are rather dull, except for the light, which is beautiful on a sunny day. One is again reminded of the Victorian's obsession with light. In fact, in spite of the extraordinary difference in style and detail, the Pennsylvania Academy and the British Museum have a great deal in common beside central planning. The lighting is from skylights in the ceiling and the ornament in the galleries is kept to a minimum so as not to compete with the art (fig. 10). In spite of Furness's penchant for bold display, he limited it to the parts of the museum where the experience was purely architectural.

Very soon the tides of taste would change again, and the Pennsylvania Academy would be seen as an anachronism. For one thing Neo-Classicism was as persistent in the United States as it was in England. But there was a further stimulus to the renewal of Greek and Roman forms in museum architecture: the Ecole des Beaux-Arts in Paris,[13] which was simply the finest architectural school in the world by the middle of the nineteenth century.

The first American to go there was Richard Morris Hunt, who later became the Vanderbilts' architect and went on to design many important buildings, including the entrance facade of the Metropolitan Museum of Art (1895) in New York. He was followed by H. H. Richardson and Louis Sullivan. Frank Lloyd Wright would have gone but didn't have the money and later thanked his lucky stars. Bernard Maybeck attended (for a short time, to be sure); his Palace of Fine Arts (1915) in San Francisco is testimony to his Beaux-Arts training. Maybeck's protege, Julia Morgan, was the first woman to be graduated from the Ecole. Among her many works for William Randolph Hearst is, of course, San Simeon, a museum of fine arts in which the newspaper tycoon found it possible to live.

The curriculum of the Ecole was loose, especially by contemporary American standards. Lectures, mainly theoretical, were given, but they were not compulsory. Examinations and work in the ateliers of experienced architects gave some unity to a young person's studies, but the various components were held together by an annual competition called the Grand Prix de Rome, in which the award was made on the basis of a student's ability to articulate the functions of a building in a logical, orderly manner around major and minor axes and then to ornament the result with mainly Baroque detail. It was in this atmosphere of French rationalism that the young Louis Sullivan, later to become one of America's greatest architects, developed his famous aphorism, "form follows function." It is also where he developed his habit, after organizing functions, of covering over the surface of his buildings with ornament in order, as Marcus Whiffen has put it, that there would be plenty to look at.[14] But the great appeal of the Beaux-Arts teaching was the organizing process.

Specifically there was in the Ecole and its teaching a particular fondness for organizing functions around a central core, or nucleus, preferably capped with a dome, off which the various facilities would be arranged in a logical manner. Such central planning characterized the design of buildings long before the nineteenth century, but the Beaux-Arts made it a creed.

There are many examples of Beaux-Arts planning in Southern California: the Riverside County courthouse, the *Herald Examiner* building, the Pasadena city hall are the first to

Fig. 9 Grand stairway, Pennsylvania Academy of the Fine Arts, Philadelphia, 1976.

Fig. 12 Grand staircase, Art Institute of Chicago, Illinois, about 1930.

Fig. 11 Walker Art Gallery, Bowdoin College, Brunswick, Maine.

come to mind. We even have our own Beaux-Arts museum in Exposition Park, the old Los Angeles County Museum of History, Science, and Art, too long forgotten except as the back-drop for a lovely rose garden and now part of the County Museum of Natural History. It was designed in 1910 by the firm of Hudson and Munsell with a florid facade and interior domed rotunda circled with marble columns. (It deserves rediscovery and restoration.)

The source of late nineteenth-century Neo-Classicism in museum design was thus, not so much England with its centrally planned British Museum, but France. One of the first Beaux-Arts museums in America was the Walker Art Gallery (1892–93) at Bowdoin College in Brunswick, Maine (fig. 11). Its designer was Charles Follen McKim, a graduate of the Ecole and one of the greatest and most fashionable American architects of the last century. A principal in the firm of McKim, Mead, and White, he freely interpreted Filippo Brunelleschi's Pazzi Chapel in Florence, setting it on a pedestal above a flight of steps and adding red brick wings to house the galleries. Inside, the architectural show was in the rotunda under the shallow dome, where the room was enriched in the arches with allegorical paintings by John La Farge, Elihu Vedder, Abbott Thayer, and Kenyon Cox, four of the most eminent American artists of the period. At the sides and back the three galleries were arranged without elaborate architectural decoration. The whole ensemble with the architectural display occurring at the entrance and the galleries almost without ornament would be prototypical of future museums.[15]

McKim, Mead, and White went on to build more elaborate museums, especially after the World's Columbian Exposition of 1893 popularized Beaux-Arts concepts of order with its theme, "The City Beautiful." Very few of the elaborate city plans that were drawn up for major cities ever got off the drawing boards, but almost every city got a new Neo-Classical civic center and an art museum in the Beaux-Arts manner. During the period between the Chicago Fair and the Great Depression most of

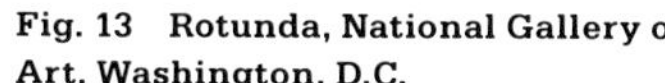

the nation's major museums were built. All of these were centrally planned and most were domed. Whether entering the Art Institute of Chicago (Shepley, Rutan, and Coolidge, 1892) or the De Young Memorial Museum in San Francisco (Louis Christian Mullgardt, 1916) or the Baltimore Gallery of Art (John Russell Pope, 1929), the same general plan was evident. The visitor went through an imposing portico, usually columned, into a reception hall with cloakroom on one side and ticket desk, usually offering postcards, on the other. If it was a two-story building, there was an elevator in the hall. Beyond was another row of columns separating the reception area from a skylit court or domed rotunda, off which ran corridors leading to galleries. This court might be extended longitudinally into atria or sculpture courts, around which other galleries were ranged. This grid could be extended indefinitely by adding quadrangles around courts and gardens.[16]

No two-story museum was without its grand staircase, usually facing the visitor upon entering the court or rotunda. The one at the Art Institute of Chicago was my introduction (fig. 12). I will never forget it. It *was* the museum as far as I was concerned. Only later did I discover that the Picassos and Impressionists were just to the left as I reached the top.

And the rotundas. Surely the greatest is the one at the old National Gallery of Art (John Russell Pope, 1941) in Washington, D.C. (fig. 13). By the time I first saw it, I had been to college and indoctrinated with the dialectic of the International Style, which told me to hate or at least to laugh at the great black marble rotunda with its statue of Mercury in the center. It took me many years to outgrow my youthful modernist prejudice.

The rotunda and the grand staircase were usually the main architectural expressions of the interior of a Beaux-Arts museum, the rest, beside perhaps corridors and courts, being neutral space that acted as a background for art. Even today, when it would seem that Beaux-Arts ideas have been left behind, the rotunda and the grand staircase persist, trans-

Fig. 13 Rotunda, National Gallery of Art, Washington, D.C.

Fig. 14 Rendering, Pavilion for Japanese Art, Los Angeles County Museum of Art.

formed, to be sure. Frank Lloyd Wright, who claimed to hate the Ecole, nevertheless adapted its principal forms in the Solomon R. Guggenheim Museum (1956), and Richard Meier consciously followed him in both his High Museum (1980–83) in Atlanta and his Museum fur Kunsthandwerk (1985) in Frankfurt. Who knows what Beaux-Arts tricks he will try at the new J. Paul Getty Museum in Brentwood? And, of course, Bruce Goff has also paid tribute to the Ecole, as well as to Wright, in his design for the Pavilion for Japanese Art (fig. 14) now being constructed to the east of the museum's Hammer Building.

Today vestiges of the Beaux-Arts style exist in tension with another great, seemingly diametrically opposed movement in architecture, the International Style, or what it is currently voguish to call "the Modern Movement." As so often happens in the history of ideas, the apparent victory of a concept, such as Beaux-Arts planning, masked a strong countercurrent of discontent with its domination. Central to the opposition was a suspicion that the tried-and-true pose of French rationalism, the Beaux-Arts's smug assumption of orderliness and its dependence on historic styles, thwarted the architect's creative instinct. The Ecole des Beaux-Arts stood for the dead hand of the past.

Taking their imagery from the modern machine, the apostles of the new would strip away ornament and style and, working from within, would create an architecture that, in the words of Le Corbusier, one of the founders of the International Style, was "a machine for living in." The truth would be naked. For museum architecture this dictum meant doing away with columns, rotundas, grand staircases, and quadrangles. Taken to its logical conclusion, it might well have limited the function of a museum to that of a chronicle of the chain of history, from which we had fortunately escaped, or it might have eliminated the museum altogether since it too was the dead hand of the past. Luckily we were spared these absurdities, probably because relatively few people ever accepted the dogma of the International Style at its most iconoclastic. Even its titans showed a romantic desire to build museums.

The International Style did have a salutary effect, focusing the attention of architects on the present condition and reordering of priorities. For museum people it meant rethinking the idea of the museum: Is its real purpose to entertain or to edify? Is its duty to the past or to the present? Is there eternal verity in the practice of the Beaux-Arts maxim that a museum should never be more than two stories tall? What is the point of rectangular galleries and exterior quadrangles? What place does individuality have in the design of a museum? Finally, how do the answers to these and many other modern questions affect museum space? The International Style challenged smug Beaux-Arts certitudes, and if its answers were too simple, the long-run effect of such questioning was to make the modern museum a considerably different and more interesting experience.

The physical embodiment of the early International Style museum was the Museum of Modern Art in New York City. Even before it erected its building on West Fifty-third Street in the late thirties, it was committed to everything that was "Cezanne and after," as the saying went at the time. The building designed by Philip Goodwin and Edward Durell Stone put the revolutionary ideas of the International Style into practice.

It is difficult for me to be objective about "the Modern." It has been so formative in my own way of looking at things. I first visited it in 1945, when it was still fairly new. At first I was shocked by its complete denial of the aesthetic of the Art Institute of Chicago, which I had known as a child. It was six stories tall and stuck in close to the sidewalk between two existing buildings (fig. 15) as if it were just another storefront. Where was the monumental entrance? The lobby was like one in an office building. Where was the grand staircase? There was a small and functional stair to the left, but its only adornment was an Alexander Calder mobile where a chandelier would have hung. At the top of the stair was a loft with only a few permanent walls. The rest, I discovered, were movable to accommodate the size and program of changing exhibitions (fig. 16). There were no galleries in the traditional sense. What to make of such a thing? The only security it offered was a sense of being in the holy place of modern art. The idea of museum was transformed. The only things that would complete the logic of elimination were freeing gallery space completely by eliminating all opaque walls and putting art in the basement. This Ludwig Mies van der Rohe, the author of the aphorism "less is more," would do in his Neue Nationalgalerie (1962–68) in Berlin.

The forties and fifties did not produce many new museums, but the old ones quickly accepted the Modern's conception of a museum with few permanent walls and opened at least some of their spaces to the more flexible manner made possible by a complex system of movable partitions. An element of surprise was

Fig. 15 Facade, Museum of Modern Art, New York, with 1951 addition designed by Philip Johnson.

Figs. 17–20 Installation views, Hammer Building, Los Angeles County Museum of Art: (upper left) *Mark Rothko, 1903–1970: A Retrospective*, July 5–September 23, 1979; (upper right) *The Russian Avant-Garde: 1910–1925*, July 3–September 28, 1980; (lower left) *German Expressionist Sculpture*, October 26, 1983–January 22, 1984; (lower right) *The Treasury of San Marco*, July 3–September 8, 1985.

added. Along with the temporary installation came another factor in the way we see art: the designer of special exhibitions as a kind of second architect. Anyone who has seen the extremely imaginative work done in the periodic transformations here at the Hammer Building must acknowledge the debt to the Modern (figs. 17–20).

If the exhibition itself was to be a work of art, it followed that much of the permanent collection must be stored so that only selected pieces pertaining to the theme of the show would be seen. It is difficult to trace this phenomenon directly to the Modern, although the staff there always realized that the very avant-garde nature of the museum made it necessary to store a large part of the collection.

The first radical employment of such weeding and highlighting came apparently in the late fifties in the galleries of the Palazzo Bianco in Genoa. My first experiences of the technique were at the Galleria Nazionale dell' Umbria in Perugia in 1961 and a week or so later in the sculpture gallery at the Terme Museum in Rome. After seeing the very best of the collections highlighted in this manner, it was strange to go on to the British Museum that year where the new "Italian look" had not yet caught on. What seemed to be thousands of Greek vases stood indiscriminately on trestles with very little interpretation offered. Five years later the spacious Duveen Gallery, designed by John Russell Pope, was opened at the British Museum, and many other galleries were renovated and freed of clutter.

The work goes on. Here in Los Angeles we are acquainted with the continuing transformation of the Southwest Museum, until recently as full of pots as the British Museum, except in this case they are Native American rather than Greek. What happened to the litter, whose general effect was confusion but whose individual pieces were precious? Many Indian artifacts are stored in the museum's Caracol Tower. Libraries can put great portions of their collections on microfilm, museums cannot. Whatever the imaginative arrangement for dealing with excess artifacts, the new exhibition procedure often requires the addition of storage space and areas where the items may be studied by scholars. So some of the social history of museum space is the fine and practical art of finding enough space—and then paying for it.

In 1943 just as museologists were digesting the many ideas that the Museum of Modern Art presented, Frank Lloyd Wright announced his plans for the Solomon R. Guggenheim Museum of Non-Objective Art in New York City. The initial reaction to his idea of a spiral ramp—he called it a chambered nautilus—was that it was highly personal, but there was nothing then like the emotional outpouring that came with its completion sixteen years later. The critics had been sold on the International Style; here was a building that contradicted it outrageously. The lesson from the Modern was that the architecture of a museum should be a sensible and, if possible, artful floor plan with space ideally being infinity, interrupted, to be sure, by the installers' tempo-

Fig. 16 Installation view, *Art in Our Time*, Museum of Modern Art, New York, May 10 – September 30, 1939.

Fig. 21 Rotunda and skylight, Solomon R. Guggenheim Museum, New York.

Fig. 22 Rotunda and skylight, High Museum of Art, Atlanta, Georgia.

rary partitions. Wright's Guggenheim indicated that he believed in the expression of space, and that expression required the manipulation of wall surfaces, fenestration, floor heights, ceiling contours, and even furniture, something that the International Style could not abide. The critics were doubly perplexed because they had already canonized Wright in his own lifetime. What to do?

The long and the short of it was to decide that the Guggenheim was a great building but a terrible museum. Wright, no admirer of the nonobjective painting that it was to hold, had forecast this judgment when he observed that people would forget the painting in their enjoyment of the architecture. I agree with Helen Searing[17] that there is no point in reiterating the negative and positive reactions to the Guggenheim, but it is important at least to note their intensity, since they are related to the critics' conception of what museum space should be. I remember, for example, James Johnson Sweeney, the director of the new museum, lecturing to a group of architectural historians in 1960, not long after the Guggenheim opened. Thinking of the leaning walls, unusual backlighting, lack of storage space, and other Wrightean niceties, he remarked that he had not yet realized the full potential that lay in the problems Wright had created. After doing some resourceful tinkering with the fabric, Sweeney resigned.

Helen Searing has observed that "for all his inventiveness, Wright has not been too proud to reach back in time and acknowledge the art museum's original heart, the domed rotunda."[18] It was in this central space that the Beaux-Arts architect could be expressive. But in his characteristic way Wright made the grand staircase (ramp) dominate the whole building (fig. 21), something that no true Beaux-Arts museum architect would ever have done. It is significant that recently Wright's ramp, with which there have been functional as well as aesthetic problems, has won admiration and its reward, emulation. In writing about his own High Museum in Atlanta, which he modestly called "a commentary on the Guggenheim Museum," Richard Meier made an extraordinarily perceptive analysis of Wright's solution of the problem before him: "The marvel of the Guggenheim is that the vertical movement provides a continual reference, not only to the central space filled with light, but to the art itself. The visitor is confronted with a multitude of ways of viewing the art. At the end of a particular exhibition, one can simultaneously see the beginning." Meier understands Wright's notions of organic unity and then goes on to suggest how he has reinterpreted Wright's ideas in his own museum: "The central problem of the Guggenheim, however, is that the ramp as gallery induces a propelling motion inappropriate to contemplation. The sloping ceilings, floors and walls are not only uncomfortable, but render the display of paintings difficult. In Atlanta we have attempted to reinterpret the particular virtues of the Guggenheim" (figs. 22–24).[19]

In developing Wright's "idea of the referent central space filled with light," Meier has developed something that is at once new and at the same time remains in touch with the Beaux-Arts tradition. His Museum fur Kunsthandwerk employs the same reinterpretation of Wright's ideas (fig. 25).[20]

In spite of Frank Lloyd Wright's excess of spirit in the Guggenheim, the very exaggeration of his visual statement provoked results outside the museum world. The fantastic image of a spiral ramp, coiling like a spring about to be released, was a welcome relief from the "less is more" banality of the International Style aesthetic of scarcity, with all its corollaries. It would not be long before Robert Venturi would declare that "less is a bore." Although Venturi criticized Wright's obsession with horizontality, apparent behind the dominant diagonal of the ramp, most people would see the Guggenheim as an example of the "complexity and contradiction" that Venturi championed[21] and one more example of the impatience with the International Style also exhibited in the contemporaneous rebellions of Eero Saarinen, Edward Durell Stone, Minoru Yamasaki, and many other architects.

Fig. 23 Installation view, Solomon R. Guggenheim Museum, New York.

Fig. 24 Installation view, High Museum of Art, Atlanta, Georgia.

Fig. 25 Interior, Museum fur Kunsthandwerk, Frankfurt, West Germany.

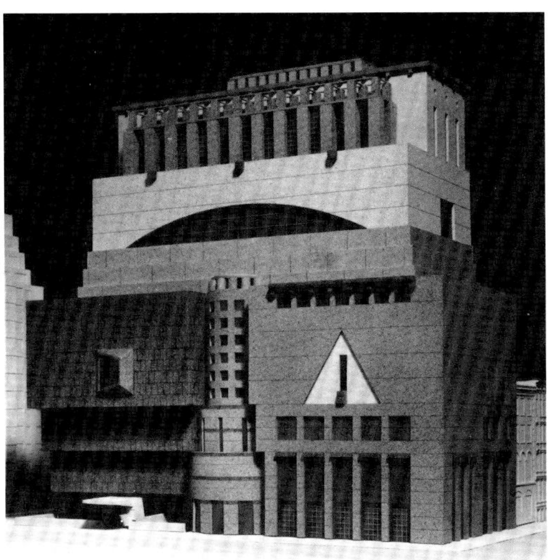

Fig. 27 Model (now superseded), facade, Whitney Museum of American Art, New York, 1985. Michael Graves, architect.

The first conspicuous reaction in museum architecture was Philip Johnson's Amon Carter Museum (1961) in Fort Worth. Ironically, Johnson, as curator of architecture at the Museum of Modern Art in the thirties, had contributed to coining the term *International Style* at an exhibition (1932) of works by Walter Gropius, Ludwig Mies van der Rohe, Le Corbusier, and other pioneers of the movement[22] whose unifying principles were antihistoricism, a love affair with the purifying model of the machine, and a desire to present the same abstraction in architecture that was being presented already in painting and sculpture. Johnson was most famous for his own Miesian glass box of a house near New Canaan, Connecticut. But now he had become tired of the International Style. The Amon Carter Museum, which he recently called "my earliest revolt from the International Style,"[23] was one of the results: another Miesian glass box, but one upon which he superimposed a facade of piers evoking the columns of Beaux-Arts architecture (fig. 26). His similar Sheldon Memorial Gallery (1963) in Lincoln, Nebraska, contains marble halls, fixed-wall galleries, and a grand staircase.

Before the full impact of a Beaux-Arts revival would be felt, another manifestation of impatience with the International Style would emerge. We have recently experienced a spirited discussion of Michael Graves's design for an expansion of the Whitney Museum of American Art in New York (fig. 27). A major point in that discussion is the fact that the Whitney, designed in 1963 by Marcel Breuer, another apostate from the International Style camp, is probably the chief monument of the Brutalist school of the sixties, at least among museums. Like the Museum of Modern Art, also remodeled and expanded over the years, it is a stack of lofts, but there the resemblance ends. Whereas those at the Modern are light and airy, those at the Whitney are dark and monumental. The ceilings, like the walls and floors, are concrete so that the light on the exhibits must generally be artificial. There are obviously benefits from such lighting, the possibility of showcasing being one of them. Islands of light dapple the prevailing darkness and can offer a pleasant overall pattern. The Oakland Museum (1968) designed by Kevin Roche, John Dinkerloo, and Associates is so low and dark that it appears that the whole museum is underground. A walk through these subterranean depths becomes a voyage of discovery of interpenetrating spaces and magnificently planted outdoor terraces (Dan Kiley, landscape architect). In the Brutalist University Museum (1970) in Berkeley, the architect, Mario J. Ciampi, following the practice of most recent museum designers, drew a kind of compromise between artificial light and natural sources.

In our study we have come around again to the concern for good lighting that deeply affects the perception of space in a museum and that has preoccupied museum designers at least since the late eighteenth century. Whereas earlier designers wanted simply to display the works of art in the best possible manner, contemporary designers have an additional problem of conservation of the artifacts, for they have discovered that all light, not just the ultraviolet rays of direct sunlight, may be destructive of some works no matter what precautions are taken. The staff of the museum's new Pavilion for Japanese Art, for example, will be rotating its exhibitions monthly in order to preserve the works for even a limited future.

The concern for the best possible lighting for seeing works of art and for their conservation has led museum architects and lighting experts to design incredibly ingenious devices usually in the ceilings of galleries, thereby adding another dimension to the experience of museum space.[24] The elaborate machinery that performs this service is not often completely visible, but its use always affects the design of the ceiling and thus the impression the architectural space.

In the eighties the architectural effects of lighting have not been limited to the galleries of museums. Anyone who has seen I. M. Pei's great hall of light in the new West Wing (1977–81) of the Museum of Fine Arts, Boston, will wonder what its function is except to make an architectural statement with its huge greenhouse on the roof. Normally there are only a few works of art in it. It is one vast space with a grand escalator at the end. One's memory is of this and not the new galleries and facilities that it has provided. Its primary function is to excite the architectural imagination of the thousands of people who come to see Boston's great collection, and it is successful.

The appeal to the masses is also an aspect of Pei's East Building (1978) of the National Gallery in Washington, D.C. The visitor is at once reminded of the sculptured space of Wright's Guggenheim, but the impression here is not of compression, but of immense, limitless space. Pei's idea is obviously to move the viewer with what the eighteenth century called the sublime, and it is successful.

The vast proportions, like the monster shows they often contain, are at once a response to the success of museums in attracting large audiences and at the same time a great democratic appeal for still larger crowds. They attempt to match in size the prestige of the art they contain. They become emblems of their cities' cultural pretensions and have been instrumental in reversing the downward economic swing of more than one city that needed a lift, aesthetic and otherwise.[25]

There are, of course, a few losses, one of them being human scale. Another is related to it: the relegation of works of art to the status of ornaments or accents to the space and a subsequent diminution of their significance as things in themselves. This phenomenon was already apparent in the Guggenheim Museum, where Wright, in his contempt for nonobjective painting, made its great Kandinsky paintings at best decorative items in the panoply of architecture.

Most architects today are not contemptuous of art. Kevin Roche solved the problem of erecting a modern museum in Georgian Williamsburg by putting it underground and surrounding it with a colonial brick fence. After all, he said, the collection was more important than the museum. But such modesty is rarely called for. Certainly I. M. Pei was sympathetic to art when he developed the space for the large Calder mobile that floats in the space near the entrance to the East Building of the National Gallery. It might even be an allusion to the memory of the one in the old staircase of the Museum of Modern Art. Likewise he gave August Rodin's sculpture of Balzac a dramatic setting, projecting the great thrust of the figure from a balcony into space. Nevertheless, surrounded by good intentions, this most dynamic sculpture since Bernini is lost in the architectural exhibitionism of the steel framing in the ceiling and the vastness of the space.

It is clear that the need for more museum space is a demand that must be met, but with superspace the old question remains, considerably enlarged: Is it possible to make a great architectural statement and at the same time serve art magnificently? Others will have their candidates for success in France, in Germany, or in the United States, but I nominate Louis I. Kahn's Kimbell Museum (1969–72) in Fort

Fig. 26 **Facade, Amon Carter Museum, Fort Worth, Texas.**

Fig. 28 Exterior, Kimbell Art Museum, Fort Worth, Texas.

Fig. 29 Installation view, *Henri Matisse: Sculptor/Painter*, May 26 – September 2, 1984, Kimbell Art Museum, Fort Worth, Texas.

Worth (fig. 28) as the greatest museum building of the twentieth century to date. The first view of it does not overwhelm. As a matter of fact, it looks like a factory. It is low with only the ripples of its multivaulted roof breaking the dominant horizontality. But when you enter the porches, whose vaults are supported only at the end corners, you realize that great architecture is coming. It is Roman as it behooves a student of Paul Cret, a graduate of the Ecole des Beaux-Arts, to make it. You enter through a forecourt (atrium-orangerie) of trees into another vaulted space, one of sixteen galleries that you will eventually encounter. As the museum expands, there will of course be more of these vaulted spaces.

Looking upward you see the lighting system. Kahn reasoned that since the collection was nineteenth century or older, it had been created in natural light and should be viewed in natural light. At the top of the vaults runs a longitudinal skylight engineered so that the light from the sun is reflected onto the sides of the concave surface whose shape was reckoned to distribute the light evenly (fig. 29). Other sources of natural light are the forecourt and three planted, inner courts that look in plan very much like the quadrangles of the historic Beaux-Arts museum. Artificial light is provided by plug-in lamps hooked to the frame of the skylight. Kahn thus brings together the loft of the International Style, the classical form and planning of the Beaux-Arts, and the technical advances of the present and gives them the personal stamp of his genius, all this while serving the art for which the museum was designed.

The Beaux-Arts, classically inspired museum is still with us. In a recent *Los Angeles Times* article on new German museums, William Wilson noted that the spaces in Stuttgart's Neue Staatsgalerie, designed by James Stirling and Michael Wilford, have been compared with the work of Karl Freidrich Schinkel, the architect of the flamboyantly Neo-Classical Altes Museum in Berlin, but added that he sensed "an Italianate enthusiasm," reminiscent of the Castel Sant' Angelo in Rome. The source is probably French. Wilson himself

points out: "Having had a vigorous work-out with the exterior, lobby, theater and cafe the architects sensibly backed off and produced an enfilade of traditional, beautifully proportioned white galleries.[26] A perfect description of the Beaux-Arts technique that Stirling repeats again in his new Arthur M. Sackler Museum at Harvard.

The construction of museums continues unabated and with some notable successes such as the small, but excellent Hood Museum designed by Charles Moore for Dartmouth College. The challenge of creating a building that is at once a sympathetic background for art and at the same time an architectural statement faces architects and museums directors with the same ambiguity that it has in the past, though they are infinitely more sensitive to its dilemma. A museum is a very difficult thing.

Notes

1. Paul Goldberger, "What Should a Museum Building Be?" *Art News* 74 (October 1975): 37. Cited by Helen Searing, *New American Art Museums* (New York: Whitney Museum of American Art, 1982), 75.
2. See, for instance, Grace Glueck, "The Art Boom Sets off a Museum Building Spree," *New York Times*, 23 June 1985; Sam Hall Kaplan, "Museums: Monuments to City Pride," *Los Angeles Times*, 30 June 1985; and William Wilson, "Germany's Grand Designs," *Los Angeles Times*, 2 November 1985.
3. Theodor Adorno, *Prisms* (Cambridge, MA.: MIT Press, 1982), 175.
4. Robert Boulanger, *Greece* (Paris: Hachette World Guides, 1964), 227.
5. I discovered this concept in Spiro Kostof, "Architecture, You and Him: The Mark of Sigfried Giedion," *Daedalus* 105 (Winter 1976): 191–92.
6. Quoted by Mordaunt Crook, *The British Museum: A Case-Study in Architectural Politics* (Harmondsworth, England: Penguin, 1972), 20.
7. Ibid., 31.
8. Ibid., 22–27.
9. Ibid., passim.
10. Illustrated, ibid., 92, 93, 107.
11. Kenneth Clark, *The Gothic Revival* (New York: Holt, Rinehart & Winston, 1928, 1962.)
12. The story is told in Searing, *New American Art Museums*, 22–23.
13. For the influence of the Ecole des Beaux-Arts in America, see [Richard Chafee], "Beaux-Arts Buildings in France and America," in Arthur Drexler, ed., *The Architecture of the Ecole des Beaux-Arts* (New York: Museum of Modern Art, 1977), 464–93.
14. Marcus Whiffen, *American Architecture since 1780* (Cambridge, MA.: MIT Press, 1969), 151.
15. Searing, *New American Art Museums*, 32–35.
16. Ibid., 35–49.
17. Ibid., 55.
18. Ibid.
19. Richard Meier, "Architect's Statement," quoted in ibid., 111.
20. See Suzanne Stephens, "Frame by Frame" and "Critique," *Progressive Architecture* 66 (June 1985): 81–91.
21. Robert Venturi, *Complexity and Contradiction in Architecture* (New York: Museum of Modern Art, 1966, 1977), 52.
22. The exhibition was simply entitled "Modern Architecture: International Exhibition." In their essay for the catalogue Philip Johnson and Henry-Russell Hitchcock lowercased *international style*, but Alfred Barr in his introduction to the catalogue capitalized the term and in so doing named the style. (See Johnson and Hitchcock, *Modern Architecture: International Exhibition* [New York: Museum of Modern Art, 1932]).
23. Quoted in Daralice Donkervoet Boles, "The Last Word," *Progressive Architecture* 65 (February 1984): 26.
24. See, for instance, "Shedding Some Light on Art," *Progressive Architecture* 65 (February 1984): 105–11, which illustrates a few of the designs that architects and lighting experts have contrived for the lighting of exhibitions and some problems they have encountered.
25. See Kaplan, "Museums."
26. Wilson, "Germany's Grand Designs."

Hardy Holzman Pfeiffer Associates

Robert Winter

The radical departure from a museum with three discrete pavilions—the Ahmanson Gallery, the Hammer Wing, and the Bing Center—separated by walkways, gardens, and in earlier days reflecting pools came in 1981 when the museum's Board of Trustees engaged the architectural firm of Hardy Holzman Pfeiffer Associates (HHPA) to reorganize the Plaza level facilities, remodel the permanent collection galleries in the Ahmanson, connect these to the Hammer by means of a bridge, and provide new gallery space for modern and contemporary art. As this multifaceted project was undertaken, it became increasingly clear that the original concept of the museum as separate entities no longer worked. The problems for curators, not to mention visitors, were many, and visually the museum had no focus. Thus, a master plan was ordered. As Earl A. Powell III, the director of the museum, has said, "The key to everything became circulation."[1] The resulting organization, including the new Robert O. Anderson Building, is thoroughly Beaux-Arts in plan if not in style.

Before the Los Angeles County Museum of Art commission HHPA had made additions to Beaux-Arts museums where their solution to the problem of style had been to become Beaux-Arts architects, conforming to the spirit if not to the letter of the styles of the classically inspired original architects. Not only was the old William Pereira plan for the Los Angeles County Museum of Art exactly the opposite of Beaux-Arts centrality, however, but the facades and interiors in their spare, if pretty, modernism were exactly the opposite of Beaux-Arts Neo-Classicism. Since the Pereira style was not assertive, there seemed to be no reason to replicate it.

In fact, in their design for the Robert O. Anderson Building, HHPA decided to capitalize on the contrast between their style and that of Pereira by playfully juxtaposing some of his decorative elements against their own glass brick, porcelain, and terra-cotta. The entrance on Wilshire, so different in its boldness from the self-effacing reticence of the older complex, is nevertheless based on the twenty-foot module of the Ahmanson entrance. The only attempt to blend the new building with the old ones was to choose Minnesota limestone for the facade because it was, in spite of not being the original material, at least harmonious with it.[2] The resulting design is not a compromise with the historical precedent of the original pavilions but a demonstration that the architects understand history and can use it in a playful discipline.

HHPA was organized in 1967 as a successor to Hugh Hardy & Associates, founded in 1962. The principals, Hugh Hardy, Malcolm Holzman, and Norman Pfeiffer, are graduates, respectively, of the schools of architecture at Princeton University, the Pratt Institute, and Columbia University. All three are fellows of the American Institute of Architects. Many of their buildings, about half of which are restorations or remodelings, have won prizes. Six before the Anderson are museums.

My first experience of a building designed by HHPA was their 1980 conversion of a 1928 theater and neighboring 1941 Montgomery Ward storefront into a civic center for the people of Madison, Wisconsin (fig. 1, overleaf). I looked at the facades of the old buildings upon which they had expended so much attention. Even as a preservationist my immediate reaction was, "Why so much bother?" By California standards the Plateresque (Spanish Renaissance) frontispiece of the theater lacked pizazz, and the storefront, while making an effort to be Georgian, had tired somewhere in the process. Surely world architecture would not have lost much if these minor relics had been bulldozed out of existence.

I changed my mind when I read Hardy's argument for the project. Rather than defending the monumental status of these facades, he pointed to their local significance. The theater, a reflection of Hollywood dreams and dreams of Hollywood, was unique in Madison; there is no other Spanish architecture there. And in this age of change, the old, Neo-Georgian Montgomery Ward store had the warmth of a familiar object. Not being sacred the building

Fig. 1 Facade, Madison Civic Center, Wisconsin.

might easily be adapted to present uses as a monument would not. Its loftlike spaces might be converted to offices and galleries.[3]

The Madison Civic Center provides insights into the work of HHPA that go beyond their theory of conversion of old buildings to new uses. As expressed by Hardy, that attitude gets into the fabric of their new buildings as well: "As architects, our firm has . . . chosen to use an architectural language that acknowledges the unlikely juxtapositions of the contemporary environment, and uses their random order to make an architecture based on awareness of disparity. Dissimilar elements are combined to form a fragmented whole more appropriate to this society than traditional concepts of order."[4]

Hardy's implied distinction between contemporary society and previous epochs may be faulty. After all, every society has been conscious of the forces of fragmentation; hence the quest for order. But he tells us what the firm is up to—the HHPA order will be complex and challenging—and gives us a means of looking at and understanding it.

An architecture rich in imagery, allusion, and contradiction requires an extraordinary grasp of the range of possible resources, a grasp, in short, of history. Confronted with the problem of incorporating an old theater and a storefront into a new building, they had to know what they were dealing with. What were their styles? HHPA would have to know history in order to get the perspective even to begin their project. But then HHPA are historians.

Their concern for the past derives from the personality and, I suspect, more strongly from the education of Hugh Hardy, who was a student at Princeton in the 1950s (as were Charles W. Moore and Robert Venturi, a significant coincidence since all three are historians, leading contemporary architects, and designers of art museums). In his biography of Moore, David Littlejohn compares the architectural school at Princeton with those at Harvard, Yale, and M.I.T. in the same period. The latter, with

Harvard under Walter Gropius in the lead, followed the Bauhaus practice of banishing history. Princeton (and the University of Pennsylvania) hung on to it, hoping to relate history to the current practice of architecture.

Hardy has written of his Princeton experience: "Architecture and art history were [taught] in the same building, McCormick Hall. . . . It is so rare for most architects even to be exposed to any history. The Beaux-Arts was still very much alive." And, he added, "No one was forcing the link-up of past and present in design classes: We just absorbed the sense of an enormously rich past."[5]

Their sensitivity to history is one reason why HHPA are in such demand for restorations of and additions to existing buildings, among the most significant being the Beaux-Arts museums at Toledo, Ohio, St. Louis, Missouri, Richmond, Virginia, and Manchester, New Hampshire. It also gives them the facility in their new work to allude to, yet not ape, the past. A good example of the most literal kind of interpretation of history, may be seen in the facade of their Best Products Company corporate headquarters building (1980) at Richmond, where a diamond pattern is picked out in clear glass brick within a wall of translucent glass (fig. 2). The idea came from the early fifteenth-century facade of the Doges Palace in Venice, where a somewhat more intricate pattern is detailed in white Istrian stone and pink marble (fig. 3). The glass brick itself is a reference to one of the characteristic devices of the

Fig. 3 Facade, Doges Palace, Venice, Italy.

Fig. 2 Facade, Best Products Company, Richmond, Virginia.

Fig. 4 Facade, Robert O. Anderson Building, Los Angeles County Museum of Art.

Streamline Moderne style of the 1930s, and in the Best Products building this is reinforced by the huge W.P.A.-era stone eagles saved from the now demolished Airlines Building (1939) in New York and reinstalled as the entrance gate. Characteristic of their creative eclecticism, surrounding the building is a medieval moat, into which fountains, reminiscent of those of the Villa d'Este at Tivoli, play. More subtle are the cornice and base of the facade, made of glazed terra-cotta, a material used in the Anderson Building as well (fig. 4), which remind the visitor of the extraordinary contribution of the terra-cotta industry to the architecture of the early twentieth century. The building is thoroughly eclectic in the true sense of the word, and yet there is nothing else like it.[6]

The firm's attitude toward the International Style is equally historicist. Nowhere do the architects deny that it existed as a style or that it is very important to them. Its ordering, clearing out, and focusing are all present in their work. Yet the International Style exists to be commented on, as another allusion; it is by no means sacred. The most obvious sign of their independence of the International Style is their attitude toward plan. In its early history practitioners of the International Style loved orthogonals, that is, the right angles in the grid of streets found in most American cities. Right angles were in. Curves were out. Diagonals were unheard of. What was important was to be clear and in that sense functional.

Sometimes HHPA play it straight, but, like their contemporary Richard Meier, they like to shift the grid, that is, impose one grid on another at a slight angle. The result is conspicuous in floor plan but not so apparent in a walk-through unless the visitor seeks it out. Nevertheless, the effect is heightened when the designer is playing with two axes and can line up walls, aisles, and furniture along one or the other.

HHPA have been called "the bad boys of architecture" because of their playfulness in shifting grids and in using inexpensive materials and because of their sense of humor about their own and other architects' work. But having fun in these areas requires a security that comes from observation and also from a constant sensitivity to where their work stands in relation to earlier work. That fun is most evident in the Madison Civic Center, which offers insight into their Anderson plan. The original Madison theater and Montgomery Ward fronted on State Street, the main commercial artery running radially from the state capitol and intersecting a north-south, east-west grid, making the site on which the civic center is built a triangle. Rapp and Rapp, the original architects, had, in fact, set the old theater interior at a 45-degree angle to the entrance, so that the grid was already shifted. It remained for HHPA to design the "crossroads," the central interior circulation space that joins their three exterior public entrances (one on each side of the triangle), serves the interior entrances, and unites the disparate buildings (fig. 5) as the Times Mirror Central Court does at the County Museum (fig. 6). The plan is the key to the style of all of the firm's buildings.

The firm's attitude toward history and plan clearly sets it apart from strict International Style dogma, but where do the architects stand in the range of modern architecture? Are HHPA "Post-Modern?"

I have assiduously avoided using that term, coined by Charles Jencks to describe recent iconoclasm in architecture,[7] because I think that its implications are as confusing as those of the term *Modern* when used to describe the International Style. But in the sense that Post-Modern suggests a freedom from the aesthetic of scarcity and its corollary, antihistoricism, certainly they are Post-Modern and in the camp often called High Tech. Like the practitioners of the International Style, High Tech architects use the machine as a model, but whereas the former take the meaning of the machine to be abstraction, the latter draw directly from the imagery of the factory and actual machinery such as ducts, metal railings, and funnels and play with them as sculpture, usually in strong color. Sometimes one does not know whether the machine parts have a

Fig. 5 Site plan, Madison Civic Center, Wisconsin, with central interior circulation space darkened.

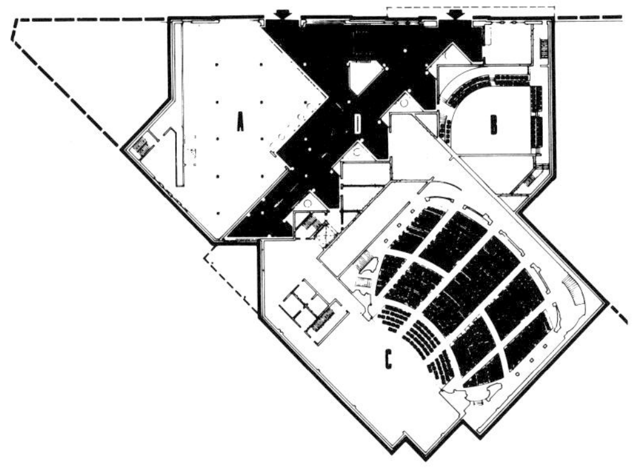

real function or have been enlisted simply in order to get a dramatic effect. In fact, as architecture critic Reyner Banham has pointed out, the work of art may resemble a power plant, but on close inspection the engineer's messy assemblage has in High Tech works been straightened out and given architectural order. Coherence not usually present in the model has been attained by the hand of art.

Obviously HHPA's work has much in common with High Tech imagery. The firm is famous for its celebration of exposed ducts and other mechanical equipment in vivid color especially in the ceiling structure: "functionalism in drag," as one admirer, Michael Sorkin, put it. Sorkin has noted, however, that the result is, not just humor, but "transcendence."[8]

HHPA's expression of materials is equally artful. By careful detailing, they make inexpensive materials look elegant, if not expensive. Their quest for raising the common to elegance is encountered especially in their use of floor coverings that tend to be taken from the kitsch culture. Everyone has had the experience of going into a hotel and immediately noticing that the carpet is badly designed and in terrible colors. Usually you shrug it off with a laugh or use it as a conversation piece over cocktails. After a while the superiority of your taste over the designer's becomes comforting, even reassuring. You begin to like what you know perfectly well is in bad taste, and it becomes part of your fondest memories of the hotel.

Banking on that perverse nostalgia, HHPA uses the most conventional products of Carpeteria to give viewers the comfort of recognition and at the same time jar them out of their easy expectations. Usually the important paths through their buildings are "paved" with cliche-ridden carpeting patterns or equally

Fig. 6 Site plan, Los Angeles County Museum of Art, with Times Mirror Central Court darkened.

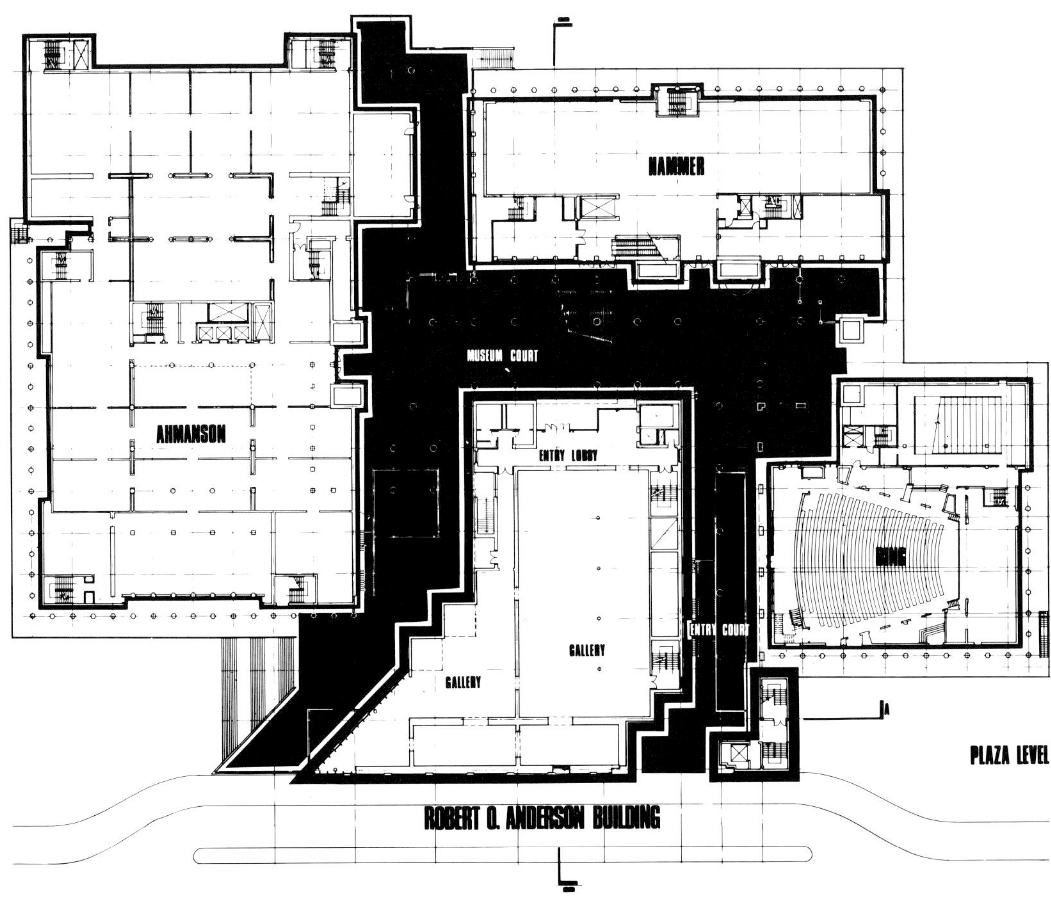

familiar black and white tiles out of 1920s lavatories. The architects call attention to the triviality of these forms and yet, posing them against patterns of great refinement, cause the viewer to see them in a new way, as in the best Pop art.

What happens to such insouciance when it is applied to art museums, whose traditions are more staid than those of administrative centers and schools? It remains but is cleaned up. Cheap carpets are replaced with good ones. Ducts are concealed. Elegant materials are used. The architects' high good humor spills over into their ideas for remodeling, but their sympathy for the ideas of the original architects of these buildings is noteworthy.

Until their commission at the Los Angeles County Museum of Art, HHPA had only worked on Beaux-Arts museum buildings. Significantly their first real museum work was to convert Andrew Carnegie's old Beaux-Arts mansion on New York's Fifth Avenue into the Cooper-Hewitt Museum (1976), an annex of the Smithsonian Institution devoted to architecture and decorative arts.[9] Carnegie's mansion had great architectural presence and thus offered serious problems to remodelers. HHPA's solution was to refurbish and enhance it, especially through new lighting, but essentially to leave it alone. As in their work on the Madison Civic Center, they are sympathetic to a building that is not a masterpiece but can be seen in a new perspective and give joy as a result.

Their second museum commission (1977) was for a remodeling of the St. Louis Art Museum, a Beaux-Arts masterpiece built in 1904 to the designs of Cass Gilbert. Over the years his great entrance hall had been filled with sculpture and bric-a-brac. It did not take long for the architects, conscious of the glories of the great space, to clear it out, leaving only the fountain at the center to act as a focal point for the room and also to point out the cross-axis through the gallery wings (fig. 7).

In the Beaux-Arts manner, they gave the architectural emphasis to the central entrance hall. Turning to the galleries, HHPA rebuilt the skylit, steel-trussed roofs, replacing the old

Fig. 7 Entrance hall, St. Louis Art Museum, Missouri.

Fig. 8 Interior during construction, Robert O. Anderson Building, Los Angeles County Museum of Art.

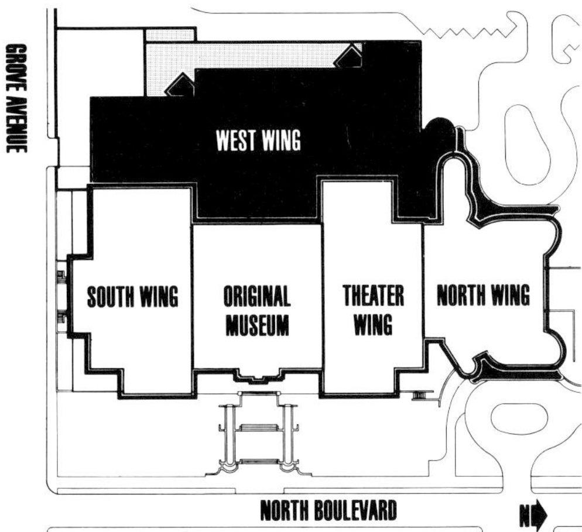

Fig. 9 Site plan, Virginia Museum of Fine Arts, Richmond.

Fig. 10 Facade, west wing, Virginia Museum of Fine Arts, Richmond.

glass with solar glass that filters out the sun's ultraviolet rays, enhancing the conservation of the art. Artificial lighting was completely renovated. With fixtures made by Jules Fisher and Paul Marantz, Inc., they bathed the classical volumes with light from new overhead sources. Always attentive to floors, they replaced the melange of materials used during previous restorations with marble. Axes were established allowing the architects to construct new openings through gallery walls in order at once to be able to see them in series, a favorite HHPA device, used in the Anderson Building too (fig. 8). Perhaps best of all, they got to build a new grand staircase.

HHPA discovered that Gilbert favored vivid colors and a rich profusion of decoration. To emphasize the architectural space, however, they opted for more muted colors, making the building read more like a Beaux-Arts rendering than a finished product. It was, as the firm described it, an "interpretive restoration."[10]

At the Currier Gallery of Art in Manchester, New Hampshire, they were faced with making additions to a Beaux-Arts building designed in 1929 by the New York firm of Tilton and Githins, good architects but by no means the equals of Cass Gilbert. As Hugh Hardy has written, "It cannot be said that Tilton's building is great or distinguished. His architecture is both too tentative and too obvious to offer a sense of discovery or wonder. Nonetheless, the Currier has a particularly American straightforward eclecticism. Besides, it is *there*, and has been The Currier for two generations."[11]

How do you hook a new building on to an old one? The International Style architect would say, "Be of your own day." Use some of the same materials in the new composition perhaps and make a few references to the proportions and lines of the original, but otherwise create something new. And, for heaven's sake, no mention of historical styles!

Freed from the dogma of the International Style aesthetic, HHPA decided to respect the integrity of the old building. The original was faced with limestone. With limestone too expensive, however, and granite too assertive, they chose a buff-colored brick that was economical and adaptable to their ideas.

Their plan required a new front door where the rear delivery entrance had been. Taking a cue from the old front entrance (now a garden entrance), they adapted its Doric order to brick and built a Palladian pavilion without monumental steps for access for the handicapped. Essentially this is a formal parking lot entrance in the manner of Los Angeles department stores, such as Bullock's Wilshire, of the twenties and thirties. There is a rightness about it which has turned a provincial museum into an architectural monument.

Their restoration of the Toledo Museum of Art (1912 and later)[12] also required the installation of a new ground-level entrance at the rear of the building. This was accomplished by making doors of five old windows and erecting a very simple canopy over them. The real work was on the interior, where a lackluster and rarely used auditorium was eliminated in order to expand exhibition space.

As in the St. Louis Museum, the remodeling offered them the opportunity to go beyond the

Beaux-Arts scheme (1910) of the original architect, Edward B. Green. The new entrance on the ground floor imposed upon them the welcome task of creating a new grand staircase that would connect the essentially new museum space to the old main axis on the floor above it. Sustaining this Beaux-Arts concept, the spacious hall opened at the ground level was walled with white Vermont marble quarried from the same site as the marble for the original building. Its floor was covered with the pink and brown marble found in the old museum, and the Verde Antique marble design at the old main entrance of the main floor was repeated. Moldings and other details were similarly replicated in the new work.

In all their remodelings—the Cooper-Hewitt, the Currier, the St. Louis, and Toledo museums—HHPA have subordinated their personal styles and predilections to the character of the earlier fabric. Hardly a lavender duct or kitsch carpet appears in any of their additions. Certainly no shifted grids. Everything has been kept within a Beaux-Arts order—with a somewhat free interpretation of Beaux-Arts details to be sure.

The project most closely resembling their extension and remodeling of the Los Angeles County Museum of Art is their recently completed expansion of the Virginia Museum of Fine Arts (1936, fig. 9). The original building was a rather bland Neo-Georgian essay erected during the Depression. Wings in similar style had been added in 1954 and 1970. A strange streamline package was added at the north in 1976. When HHPA was asked to design a west wing that would supplement the gallery space and provide a new entrance, the firm composed a facade that echoed the proportions of the original (fig. 10) with its later wings, even repeating the shadow patterns of its bays, but omitting its pediments, balustrades, and other Georgian details. The effect is decidedly contemporary and at the same time harmonious with the disparate parts of the older building.[13]

It will be apparent to everyone that in creating the Robert O. Anderson Building HHPA has employed almost all the design principles that characterize their earlier buildings: they brought three old facilities together into a coherent system with potential for addition, taking ideas from the old buildings, exposing them, and giving them a new context providing a complex disposition of parts. Whether the resulting congeries is another of their many successes, only time will tell.

Notes

1. Earl A. Powell III, interview with the author, 3 January 1986.
2. Norman Pfeiffer, interview with the author, 24 April 1986.
3. Hugh Hardy, "It Is Wrong to Preserve Old Buildings Academically and Scientifically as Yesterday's Stage Sets. . . ." *Architectural Record* 162 (August 1977): 91.
4. Hugh Hardy, "An Architecture of Awareness for the Performing Arts," *Architectural Record* 145 (March 1969): 119–20.
5. Quoted in David Littlejohn, *Architect: The Life and Work of Charles W. Moore* (New York: Holt, Rinehart and Winston, 1984), 118–19.
6. See David Morton, "Best Bets," *Progressive Architecture* 62 (February 1981): 66–73.
7. Charles Jencks, *The Language of Post-Modern Architecture* (New York: Rizzoli, 1977).
8. Michael Sorkin, *Hardy Holzman Pfeiffer* (New York: Whitney Library of Design, 1981), 8–9.
9. Hardy, "It Is Wrong," 92.
10. Ibid., 91–92; and Mildred F. Schmertz, "Hardy Holzman Pfeiffer Re-establish the Themes of a Great Beaux-Arts Building," *Architectural Record* 163 (October 1978): 85–87, 94–95.
11. Hugh Hardy, "Expanding an Eclectic Art Gallery for a New Era of Use," *Architectural Record* 170 (August 1982): 101–11.
12. David Morton, "Class Distinctions," *Progressive Architecture* 64 (August 1983): 66–71.
13. See Helen Searing, *New American Art Museums* (New York: Whitney Museum of American Art, 1982), 114–21.

ANGELES COUN
FOUNDING
DANGER
KEEP OUT

Construction Documentation

Photographs by Tim Street-Porter

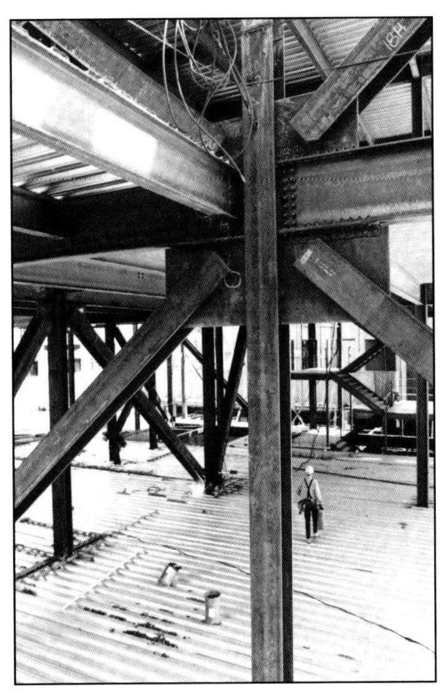

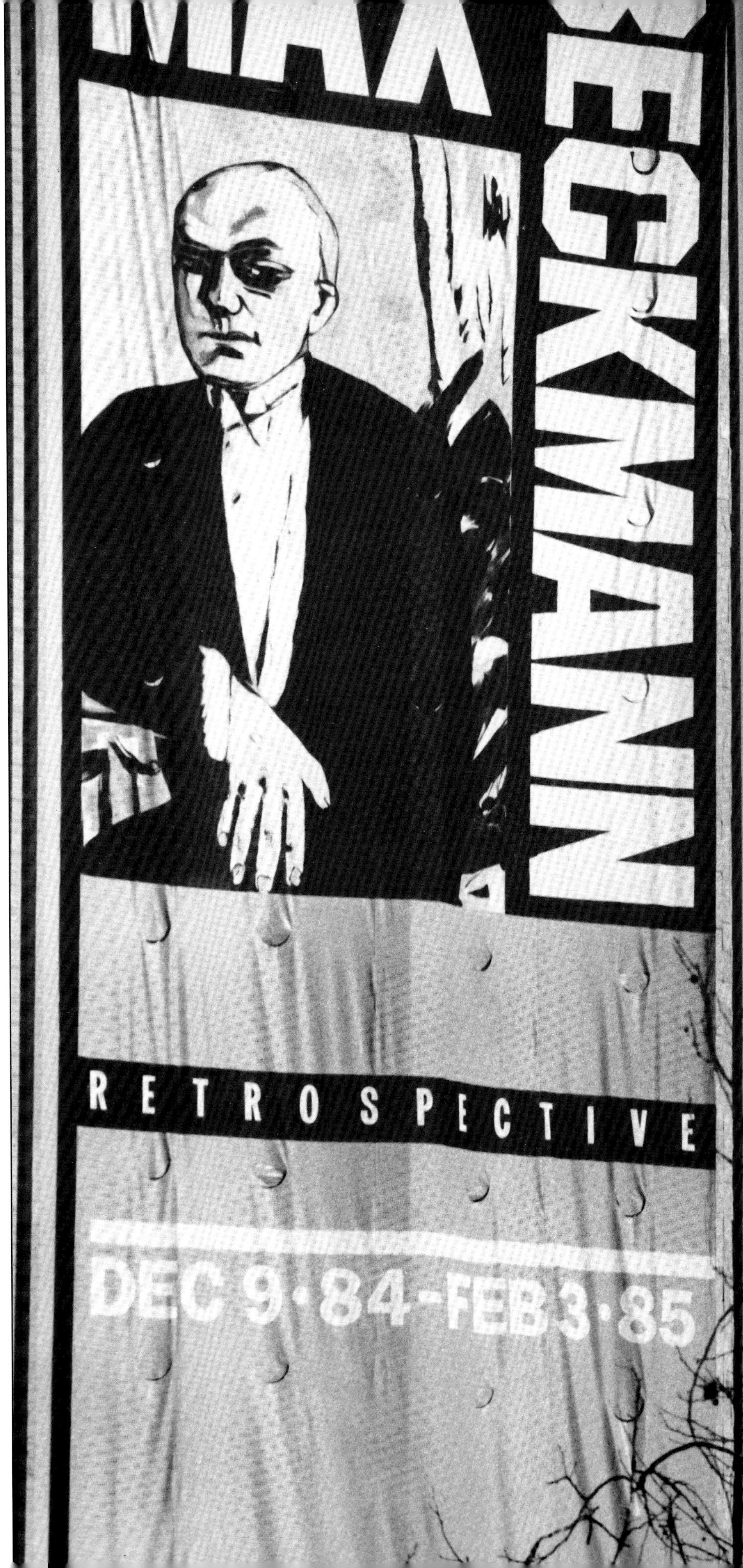
MAX
ECKMANN
RETROSPECTIVE
DEC 9·84–FEB 3·85

280C
2112
A325

Project Data
Construction and Materials

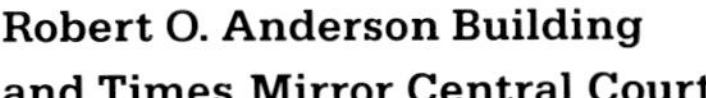

Robert O. Anderson Building and Times Mirror Central Court

The Robert O. Anderson Building is a 115,200-square-foot structure located at the front of the museum complex on Wilshire Boulevard. It provides more than 50,000 square feet of gallery space for special exhibitions and for the museum's permanent collection of twentieth-century art. This includes approximately 18,500 square feet on the Plaza level for special exhibitions as well as more than 14,000 square feet on the second level for art of recent decades and approximately 17,000 square feet on the third level for art from the turn of the century through the years following World War II. The lower level is reserved for administrative functions.

The Anderson facade is three hundred feet long and steps up to a height of one hundred feet. The building's western most edge is terraced at the Plaza and second levels to provide areas for the installation of large outdoor sculpture. A setback of forty feet from the street accommodates a visitor drop-off area on Wilshire Boulevard.

The expansion program, of which the Anderson construction is the major part, includes the creation of a new Wilshire Boulevard entrance for the entire museum complex. This monumental portal, fifty feet wide and as high as a five-story building, leads visitors to a grand twenty-foot-wide stairway, flanked by a four-tiered waterfall cascading from the Times Mirror Central Court into a pool at street level. Six large terra-cotta-veneered columns support skylights seventy feet above. The waterfall is flanked by a granite Donors' Wall.

The stairway leads to the Times Mirror Central Court. This grand public space, three stories high, serves as the focus and orientation point for the entire museum complex. The partially roofed court covers nearly an acre and is bounded by the museum's four buildings: the Ahmanson Building to the west, the Hammer Building to the north, the Bing Center to the east, and the Anderson Building to the south. The Central Court includes a new admissions and information kiosk. The Museum Shop has been relocated under the Hammer Bridge at the court's northwest end.

Total new or renovated area:	275,000 square feet
Robert O. Anderson Building:	115,200 square feet
W.M. Keck Foundation Gallery:	8,500 square feet
Times Mirror Central Court:	40,000 square feet
Center for Education:	14,800 square feet
Conservation Center:	72,000 square feet
Doris Stein Research and Design Center for Costumes and Textiles:	1,200 square feet
East and West Gardens:	51,000 square feet
Environmental Control Center:	10,000 square feet
Museum Shop:	3,500 square feet
Pavilion for Japanese Art:	32,100 square feet
Robert Gore Rifkind Center for German Expressionist Studies:	2,800 square feet

Construction features of the Robert O. Anderson Building and Times Mirror Central Court

Foundation

A mat-type foundation was required to distribute the weight of the building over subsurface silts, clay, and sand impregnated with asphalt. Consisting of five thousand cubic yards of steel-reinforced structural concrete, the mat was set down in one continuous ten-and-one-half-hour pour, the largest concrete pour in Los Angeles in seventeen years. The thickness of the mat varies from three to eight feet. A special gas collection system has been engineered to alleviate any potential methane buildup associated with the La Brea Tar Pits.

Superstructure

The building's steel structure is braced in a number of areas to provide the rigid frame required for seismic stability. The ground floor is a composite of a corrugated steel deck and three inches of concrete topping. All structural components are fireproofed. There are approximately 940 tons of structural steel in the Anderson Building and 28 tons of structural steel in the Times Mirror Central Court.

Minnesota stone

The principal cladding on the Wilshire Boulevard elevation is Northern Pink Buff Minnesota stone, a type of limestone with veins of magnesium carbonate, quarried by the Vetter Stone Co. in Mankato, Minnesota. It was chosen because it harmonizes with the color of the

museum's original buildings. The stone is veine cut to reveal the layered sediments and has a sandblasted tapestry finish. It is typically three to four inches thick and is attached to the structure in rectangular slabs ranging from one foot four inches by two feet to two feet eight inches by five feet. The slabs are carved to provide vertical indentations and protrusions along the facade, subtly echoing various elements in the design of the original buildings.

Glass block and brick

Bands of glass block, in combination with interior louvers, permit natural daylight to enter south-facing galleries at each level. Some are designed to match the carved configurations of the surrounding stone. An ultraviolet filter in the glass limits the light entering the galleries; a denser filter limits the heat gain at the orientation and office areas. Each block has a surface area eight by eight inches square. Molded green glass bricks are used at forty-five- and ninety-degree-angle corner areas, where ordinary glass blocks could not be used. Due to weight limitations in pouring and setting molten glass, these bricks are made in two pours; a hairline joint can be seen in each brick. The glass blocks and glass bricks were manufactured by the Pittsburgh Corning Co., Pennsylvania.

Terra-cotta bands

Horizontal bands of terra-cotta are incorporated in the Wilshire Boulevard facade using profiled sections developed by the architect especially for this project. The standard pieces, one foot four inches by two feet, are extruded baked clay with a multicolored, greenish glaze. Handmade pieces are used to provide indentations and protrusions that match the vertical patterns of the stone and glass block. Terra-cotta is also used to clad the columns in the Times Mirror Central Court and along the entrance stairway. All the terra-cotta pieces were manufactured by the Gladding McBean Co., Lincoln, California.

Porcelain panels

The building is sheathed on its east, north, and west elevations in four-by-eight-foot steel panels with an off-white porcelain enamel coating.

The panels are slightly curved, or "pillowed," in order to avoid the visual effect that occurs with the slipwarping, or "oil canning," of flat panels. Panels at the lower levels of the building have been acoustically treated. The panels were manufactured by Cameo (California Metal Enameling Co.) in Los Angeles.

Skylights	The skylights above the entrance and Times Mirror Central Court are composed of Kalwall (approximately 14,000 square feet) and strips of glass (approximately 4,400 square feet). Kalwall is a translucent plastic panel of high insulating and fire protection value manufactured by the Kalwall Corp. of Manchester, New Hampshire. (It will be the principal material used for the exterior walls of the museum's Pavilion for Japanese Art, opening early 1988.) Kalwall with a light-transmitting value of only 3 percent is used in the west-facing skylights to reduce heat gain in the Central Court. Kalwall with a light-transmitting value of 17 percent, along with glass strips, are used in east-facing skylights. The skylights of the Central Court provide an "umbrella" for the grand public space—open-air, yet protected. Overhangs of the skylights at their open ends provide protection from wind-driven rain.
Entrance curtain wall	The entrance to the Anderson Building from the Times Mirror Central Court is a curtain wall of three-quarter-inch-thick clear tempered glass. The glass is supported by horizontal aluminum mullions. The entry doors are also three-quarter-inch-thick tempered glass.
Windows	Windows facing Wilshire Boulevard and the Times Mirror Central Court are glazed in clear one-and-one-quarter-inch insulating glass, which is tempered and laminated.
Glass skylights	Third-floor galleries have clear glass skylights facing north to allow natural light to enter these rooms. Louvers in the ceilings of these galleries and translucent panels above them diffuse the natural light and direct it to the wall surfaces.

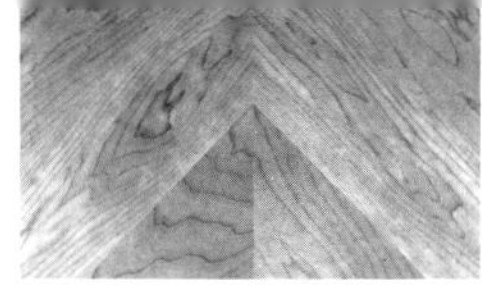

Ceiling heights

Ceiling heights in the galleries vary from sixteen and a half to eighteen feet for a wide range of installation and lighting requirements. The orientation area at the southwest corner of the building is a two-story space with a ceiling height of nearly forty feet.

Gallery walls

Gallery walls are made of standard wallboard with a special fire retardant plywood backing. This sturdier-than-usual wall permits the installation of works of art of great size and weight.

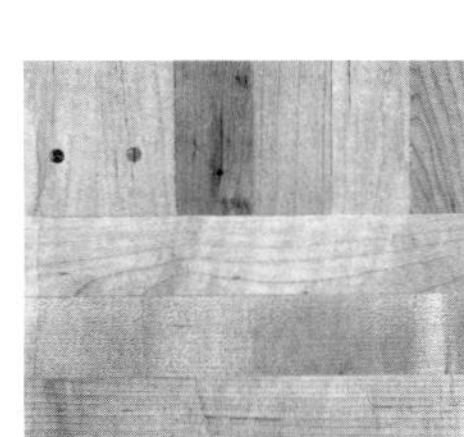

Gallery floors

Because floors in the special exhibition galleries at the Plaza level are carpeted, it is possible to erect and remove temporary walls without having to plug and sand the floors between installations. The parquet floors in the permanent collection galleries are of light maple. Floors at the third level are carpeted and have a maple strip border.

Public stair

The stair rising from the second floor in the orientation area at the southwest corner of the Anderson Building is a combination of painted steel, brass, and stone. The stair treads are of Notre Dame marble quarried in France.

Elevators

Three new elevators—one at the Wilshire Boulevard entrance for handicapped visitors, a passenger elevator in the Times Mirror Central Court, and a service elevator for the Anderson Building—are provided. The service elevator cab, with an eighteen thousand-pound capacity, is nine feet two inches wide, fourteen feet high, and sixteen and a half feet deep. The door opens to a width of six feet ten inches and a height of ten feet ten inches to accommodate a large variety of artworks.

Security systems

An expansion of the existing Honeywell security and fire protection system, designed especially for the museum, provides the sophisticated monitoring and controls for the Anderson Building. Components include motion detectors, microphones, closed circuit television, intrusion alarms, automatic locking devices, smoke and heat detectors, patrol tour stations, annunciation and control panels, communication stations, and speakers.

Temperature and humidity control	Enviromental systems are designed to maintain seventy-two degrees Fahrenheit and 55 percent relative humidity throughout the building at all times. Control accuracy is within two degrees Fahrenheit and 2 percent relative humidity.
Court paving	The Times Mirror Central Court is paved with three types of granite and broom-finished concrete. The granite is as quarried by the Cold Spring Granite Co., Cold Spring, Minnesota, in Sierra White, Cold Spring Green, and Academy Black with a thermal finish, that is, a slightly abrasive texture that does not becomes slippery when wet. The granite patterns lead the visitor through the entrance and emphasize the axial relationships of the museum's buildings. Multicolored medallions of granite are located at the entrance to each building.
Donors' Wall	The Donors' Wall is clad in Cold Spring Green granite with a polished finish. Donors' names were sandblasted into the stone at the quarry.

Design team

Architect:	Hardy Holzman Pfeiffer Associates
Owner's representative:	Project Control, Inc.
Structural engineer:	S. B. Barnes and Associates
Mechanical/electrical engineer:	Hayakawa Associates
Lighting consultant:	Jules Fisher and Paul Marantz, Inc.
Acoustical consultant:	Peter George Associates
Geotechnical engineer:	Leroy Crandall and Associates
Civil engineer:	Rogoway/Borkovetz Associates
Landscape architect:	Hanna/Olin Ltd.
Vertical transportation:	Lerch Bates and Associates
Museum Shop consultant:	Museum Quality Services
Graphic and signage systems:	Carbone/Smolan
Contractor:	Turner Construction Co.

Selected Works in the Twentieth-Century Art Collection

Stephanie Barron
Curator of Twentieth-Century Art

The collection of twentieth-century art has expanded greatly since the museum moved to Hancock Park and continues to grow ever more rapidly. The seventy-five works illustrated here, including some gifts promised on the occasion of the opening of the Robert O. Anderson Building, illustrate only a part of the more than eight hundred objects in the collection. These include important holdings in German Expressionism, modern sculpture, and Abstract Expressionism. There are outstanding examples of Cubism, Dada, Surrealism, De Stijl, and European modernism that rank among the finest achievements of Braque, Matisse, Schwitters, Magritte, and Mondrian. Our extensive collection of California painting and sculpture of the past two decades represents an overview of the achievement of this region, and our impressive holdings from Frank Stella's entire career are particularly noteworthy.

All the works illustrated here entered the collection in the past forty years. Nearly 40 percent of them came from the bequest of David E. Bright or through the continuing generosity of the Modern and Contemporary Art Council. Other benefactors whose gifts of art and acquisition funds have notably enhanced the twentieth-century art collection include Anna Bing Arnold, the Michael and Dorothy Blankfort Collection, B. Gerald Cantor, George Gard De Sylva, the Art Museum Council, and the National Endowment for the Arts. As we approach the twenty-first century, the museum will grow and mature only with the ongoing generosity and commitment of collectors and donors of acquisition funds.

Prior to installation in the Anderson Building all works of twentieth-century art underwent thorough examination in the museum's Conservation Center.

1900 – 1920: The Figure

1

3

4

2

7

6

The prodigious career of the Spanish artist Pablo Picasso began with the Blue Period, the first works in a style recognizably his own. Much Blue Period painting breaks with traditional portraiture by emphasizing bold simplification, penetrating psychological observation, and intense coloration. *Portrait of Sebastián Juñer Vidal*, 1903 (no. 1), conveys a sense of the sitter's isolation and suffering. Such gaunt figures owe much to the angularity and attentuated forms of El Greco's paintings, which had been rediscovered at the turn of the century. ■ Henri Matisse's liberating use of color became one of the major influences in modern art. His paintings seen at the 1905 Salon d'Automne in Paris triggered the critical appelation *fauve* (wild beast) because it seemed he applied his riotous colors without regard to subject. Matisse was soon joined by others, including André Derain and Maurice Vlaminck (no. 2), whose paintings were also Fauve in spirit. The boldly simplified figure of Matisse's *Standing Male Nude,* 1900 (no. 3), defined by heavy outlines and exaggerated contours, anticipates his Fauve paintings by nearly five years. ■ Matisse is known for his sculpture as well as for his painting, some of which he

5

created in series. *Heads of Jeannette*, 1910–13 (no. 4), traces the journey from traditional portraiture, reminiscent of the nineteenth century, to stylization, influenced by primitive art, and ultimately to abstraction from nature. ■ Matisse's work, like that of most of his French colleagues, was relatively unaffected by World War I. *Tea* (no. 5), his grand painting of 1919, marks the beginning of his postwar phase. This seemingly conventional scene, set in his garden near Paris, provided him the occasion to explore the physiognomy of his sitters. In particular, the face of the woman on the right, his daughter, Marguerite, is distorted in a strikingly Cubist-like and evocative manner. In this sense *Tea* is a logical development from *Heads of Jeannette*. ■ Prewar Russian avant-garde painters like Mikhail Larionov experimented with Fauve-like painting known as Neo-Primitivism. *Dancing Soldiers*, 1909–10 (no. 6), epitomizes their crude brushwork, flattened perspective, and low-life subjects. ■ Marc Chagall's *Violinist in the Snow*, c. 1912 (no. 7), depicts one of his familiar subjects, here shown with powerful color, expressively deformed line, and customary disparity of scale.

Cubism and Abstraction

8

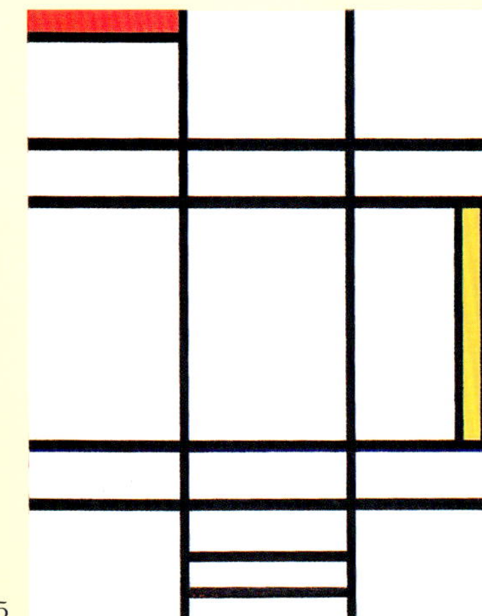

15

9

10

It was Cubism, developed in France by Picasso and Georges Braque, which radically altered pictorial space and influenced a generation of artists in Paris. In their portraits and still lifes of 1910–14, the Cubists reduced form to the interaction of planes on the picture surface. Braque's oval *Still Life with Violin*, 1914 (no. 8), is a masterful example of this radical change in picture making. The space is absolutely frontal, marking Cubism's complete break with Renaissance perspective. Alexander Archipenko created a small group of multimedia reliefs when he was in Paris from 1908 to 1917. These he called sculpto-paintings. *Woman with Hat*, 1916 (no. 9), is a rare example of this type of polychromed Cubist sculpture. Fernand Léger's *The Disks*, 1918–19 (no. 10), similarly illustrates Cubism's "simultaneous vision" (objects seen from several vantages at once). In this consideration of the Machine Age, Léger's rhythmic juxtaposition of color, form, and surface conveys the texture of modern city life. ■ The revolutionary turmoil of the decade 1910–20 changed the face of Europe and the world. The art of the period must be seen in this context. An urge to move away from representation toward abstraction emerged simultaneously in several countries as artists sought to transmit prevalent philosophical, spiritual, and scientific ideas. In his book

11

16

13

12

14

Concerning the Spiritual in Art Wassily Kandinsky, one of the leading thinkers in the development of nonobjective painting, argued for pictorial expression independent of naturalistic representation. ■ The Czech painter František Kupka, another pioneer of abstract painting, was versed in the effects colors produce on their neighbors. In *Irregular Forms: Creation*, 1911 (no. 11), Kupka attempted a plastic parallel with the dynamics of the cosmos, freed from an identifiable site and relying on abstract form and color. ■ From the beginning abstraction followed two courses: the organic, expressionistic abstraction of prewar Kandinsky and the structured abstraction of Russian avant-garde artists, such as Alexandr Rodchenko (no. 12) and El Lissitzky (no. 13), Bauhaus artists in Germany, like Kandinsky (no. 14), and the Dutch De Stijl painter Piet Mondrian (no. 15). In Germany in 1919 Kurt Schwitters, influenced by the Cubists, who pioneered collage by introducing objects from the world around them into their paintings, developed his *Merz* collage by assembling detritus in the spirit of the "antiart" Dada into new structures (no. 16).

German Expressionism

18

17

19

23

The German Expressionist movement began with two artists' groups: Die Brücke (the Bridge) in Dresden in 1905 and Der Blaue Reiter (the Blue Rider) in Munich in 1911. Die Brücke was founded by four young architectural students—Ernst Ludwig Kirchner, Karl Schmidt-Rottluff (no. 17), Erich Heckel, and Fritz Bleyl—who proclaimed their passion for art and their desire to free themselves from society's conventions. In African and Oceanic art, of which the Dresden Ethnological Museum had an outstanding collection, they found some of the expressive techniques they sought. *Two Women,* 1911/22 (no. 18), an aggressive portrait, depicts Kirchner's wife, Dodo (right), with audacious color and bold forms, characteristics that are among Die Brücke's major contributions to the history of modern art. Kandinsky and Franz Marc were the founders of Der Blaue Reiter, which strove to develop nonobjective art. In 1912 they published an almanac, *Der Blaue Reiter*, one of the most important publications of modern art. Among the earliest abstract paintings are Kandinsky's series of works with titles reminiscent of musical forms—Improvisations (no. 19), Impressions, Compositions—in which color and shape are his subjects rather than his means. ■ Artists in this period especially in Germany were expressing their presentiments of war.

20

21

22

24

In Berlin in 1913 Ludwig Meidner painted apocalyptic landscapes in which earth and sky appear rent with volcanic fury (no. 20). After the war several short-lived radical artists' groups emerged which were active during the November Revolution and the Weimar Republic. Otto Dix executed a group of imposing, forcefully colored mythological subjects, including *Leda*, 1919 (no. 21), when he was active with the Dresden group Secession 1919. ■ The German Expressionists were known for their sculpture as well as for their painting and experiments in printmaking. Ernst Barlach's works from 1906 until 1937 give form to the most fundamental human suffering: hunger, death, and grief. In *The Beggar*, 1930 (no. 22), heavy garments prevent details from disturbing formal unity. *The Beggar* was one of sixteen figures intended for the facade of the St. Katherinenkirche in Lübeck. ■ Almost all the Brücke artists carved wood sculptures. Kirchner is said to have made almost one hundred. After the war he moved to Switzerland, where he inspired a group of young Swiss artists to form Rot-Blau (Red-Blue). The leading members of the group, Herman Scherer (no. 23) and Albert Müller (no. 24), created ambitious wood sculptures inspired by Kirchner.

European Dada and Surrealism

28

26

29

25

27

If a single work of art can represent an entire movement, René Magritte's *The Treachery of Images*, c. 1928–29 (no. 25), typifies Surrealism. The meticulously rendered pipe above the seemingly contradictory legend, *"Ceci n'est pas une pipe"* (This is not a pipe), confounds pictorial realism. Magritte's "lie" bespeaks a deeper truth: this indeed is not a pipe but the *picture* of a pipe. Thus Magritte sweeps aside all comfortable notions about subject matter and deals with the duality of meaning, the difference between image and word. ■ The juxtaposition of disparate objects is also the basis of Picasso's whimsical *Centaur*, 1955 (no. 26), composed of photographic equipment and other "found" items used in the documentary film *The Mystery of Picasso* (1955). Combined in this unusual way, they take on new meaning. ■ Dadaist Marcel Duchamp was an innovator among artists appropriating common objects for art. His *Box in a Valise*, 1955–68 (no. 27), is a "portable museum" of seventy-one of his works—some reproduced on celluloid or fine paper, others miniaturized—all fitted into a leather valise, conceptually encapsulating his career.

The New Abstraction

31

30

32

33

"As I paint, the first stage is free and unconscious, the second stage is carefully calculated," wrote the Surrealist Joan Miró. In *Animated Forms*, 1935 (no. 30), he captures the spontaneity of the first stage, reminiscent of his 1920s experiments with automatic writing. American abstraction of the early 1940s, especially that of Arshile Gorky (no. 31), owes much to the example of European Surrealists, many of whom were exiled in New York during World War II. ■ Jackson Pollock also derived his mature style from Surrealism, automatism, and images drawn from the subconscious. He covered his unprimed canvas with quick-drying paint, which he worked from all sides (no. 32). His approach was a deliberate break with traditional painting. By limiting his palette, he obtained dynamic tension from the skeins of black and white that swirl across the canvas with all the force of the artist's emotion. ■ In the 1950s New York supplanted Paris as the center of contemporary art. The way American painters approached, even attacked, their canvases allowed their audiences to "witness" the creative process. In America this new art was called Abstract Expressionism; in France, Art Informel or Art Brut. Jean Dubuffet (no. 33) sought inspiration in nontraditional sources, evoking organic forms, graffitilike drawing, and crude materials.

Abstract Expressionism

36

42

34

35

39

For Franz Kline, a leading American Abstract Expressionist painter, the polarity of black and white best expressed the thrusting diagonals that characterize his style (no. 34). His surging brushstrokes, made with quick-drying enamels, generate remarkable effects in density and surface. Landscape inspired several painters in the fifties, including Willem de Kooning, working in New York, and Richard Diebenkorn in California. Powerful and expansive paintings, such as de Kooning's *Montauk Highway*, 1958 (no. 35), seem to blaze like beacons across the land. His broad, sweeping brushstrokes and suggestion of the dynamism of urban life are not unlike Kline's. Diebenkorn's composition (no. 36) is more calligraphically rendered, with patches of radiant color reflecting the artist's feelings about his native West. Helen Frankenthaler's paintings of the late fifties (no. 37) indicate her awareness of Pollock's all-over canvases but retain the lightness and transparency of touch that has characterized her work for several decades. Working directly on unprimed canvas, as did Morris Louis (no. 38), she created washes, or stains, of irregular dimensions that appear organic in nature. ■ Soft-edged, symmetrically arranged rectangles of glowing, atmospheric color in paintings such as *White Center*, 1957 (no. 39), made Mark Rothko a

40

38

37

41

major figure in color-field painting. Despite this painting's large scale, its colors envelope the viewer intimately. ■ Abstract Expressionist sculpture shares with painting a reliance on powerful line, constructed shape—frequently incorporating found objects or industrial materials—and occasional punctuations of color. Some, like Isamu Noguchi's *Cronos*, 1947 (no. 41), are large-scale organic compositions relating to European Surrealism. David Smith was foremost among American sculptors. Influenced by Cubism and by Picasso's constructed sculpture, Smith's Cubi series (no. 42) comprises rhythmic, inventively conceived geometric frameworks, distinguished by their burnished steel surfaces. Truly modern sculpture, the "stride" of the Cubi, a metaphor for walking, is not grounded by any base or support.

The Sixties: Assemblage and Pop

43

44

45

46

47

Common objects, recognizable images, and assembled narrative compositions, preoccupations of twentieth-century artists as diverse as Schwitters, Picasso, Duchamp, and Max Ernst, continued as the subjects of sculptors in the 1960s. The Surrealists' exploration of the poetic transformations that result when objects are oddly contextualized influenced both Lucas Samaras's and H. C. Westerman's work. Ambivalence and opposition underlie Samaras's tantalizing, yet repellent pin-covered boxes (no. 43). Westerman, delighting in visual and verbal puns, relies on words and beautifully crafted images to convey his meaning (no. 44). ■ The art of assemblage (construction of new objects from exisiting ones) traces back to Duchamp. Los Angeles produced several assemblage artists in the late fifties and sixties, key among them Edward Kienholz (nos. 45–46), whose infamous *The Back Seat Dodge '38*, 1964, when exhibited at the museum in 1966 created a county-wide debate on pornography versus art and the public mandate regarding morality versus professional art expertise. ■ Of the American artists whose startling transformations of commercial imagery became known in the 1960s as Pop art, the work of Claes Oldenburg, Roy Lichtenstein, Andy Warhol, and George Segal best exemplify the style. Oldenburg's *Giant Pool Balls*,

48

51

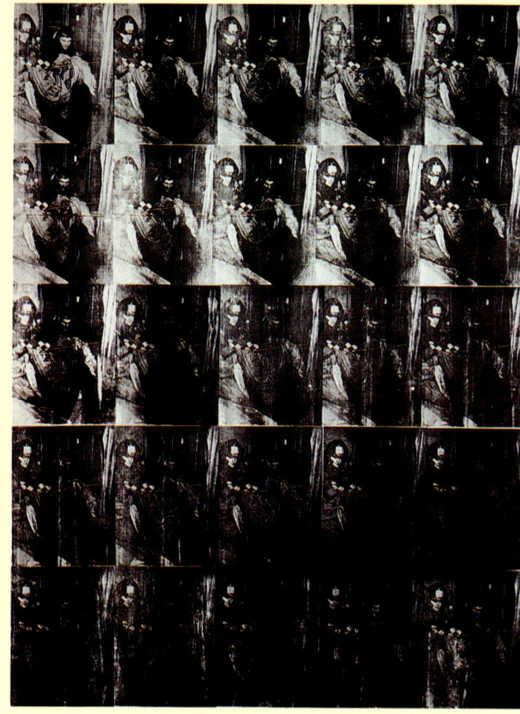
49

50

1967 (no. 47), is one of the overscaled, hard objects that the artist began making in 1962 and one of the most literally represented. Lichtenstein adopted comic strip imagery and mechanical reproduction processes (ben-day dots) (no. 48) to create a personal style of contrasting, but compatible forms. Warhol rendered his Disaster paintings (no. 49) in part by "cheap" silkscreening, which appears to contradict the grimness of the images he has chosen and the seriousness of his social concern. Segal chose familiar figures in unremarkable poses (no. 50) that, through the casting process, achieve a kind of universality. In *Actual Size*, 1962 (no. 51), Ed Ruscha contrasts the accidental drips and splatters of Abstract Expressionism and the control and contrivance of the "label" in the upper portion of the painting.

Ceramics and Glass

52

53

54

55

Los Angeles in the fifties and sixties was the setting for explorations in materials, not least of which was a revival of clay as a sculptural medium. Peter Voulkos and John Mason rebelled against the hierarchical division of media and began to view clay in terms of its own merits. Voulkos was the first to free the medium from its small scale and decorative and functional connotations. He was joined by Mason (no. 52) at the Otis Art Institute, where they influenced other artists, among them Billy Al Bengston and Kenneth Price. These artists sought to rediscover the essential characteristics of clay as a plastic material. In 1972–77 Price created *Happy's Curios* (no. 53), an environment that consists of numerous ceramic units inspired by Mexican and Southwest imagery. ■ Robert Arneson, working in Northern California, combines satire and humanism in monumental ceramic sculpture. Composed of bricks and glazed forms, they frequently comprise self-portraits with references to history (no. 54). ■ Glass too has been reevaluated recently as a sculptural medium. Inspired by Venetian glassmakers, Dale Chihuly has been creating luminous, delicately colored compositions since the 1960s. He stacks glass vessels to create more complex pieces. The baskets of Northwest Coast Indians influenced *Seaform*, 1981 (no. 55).

Minimalism

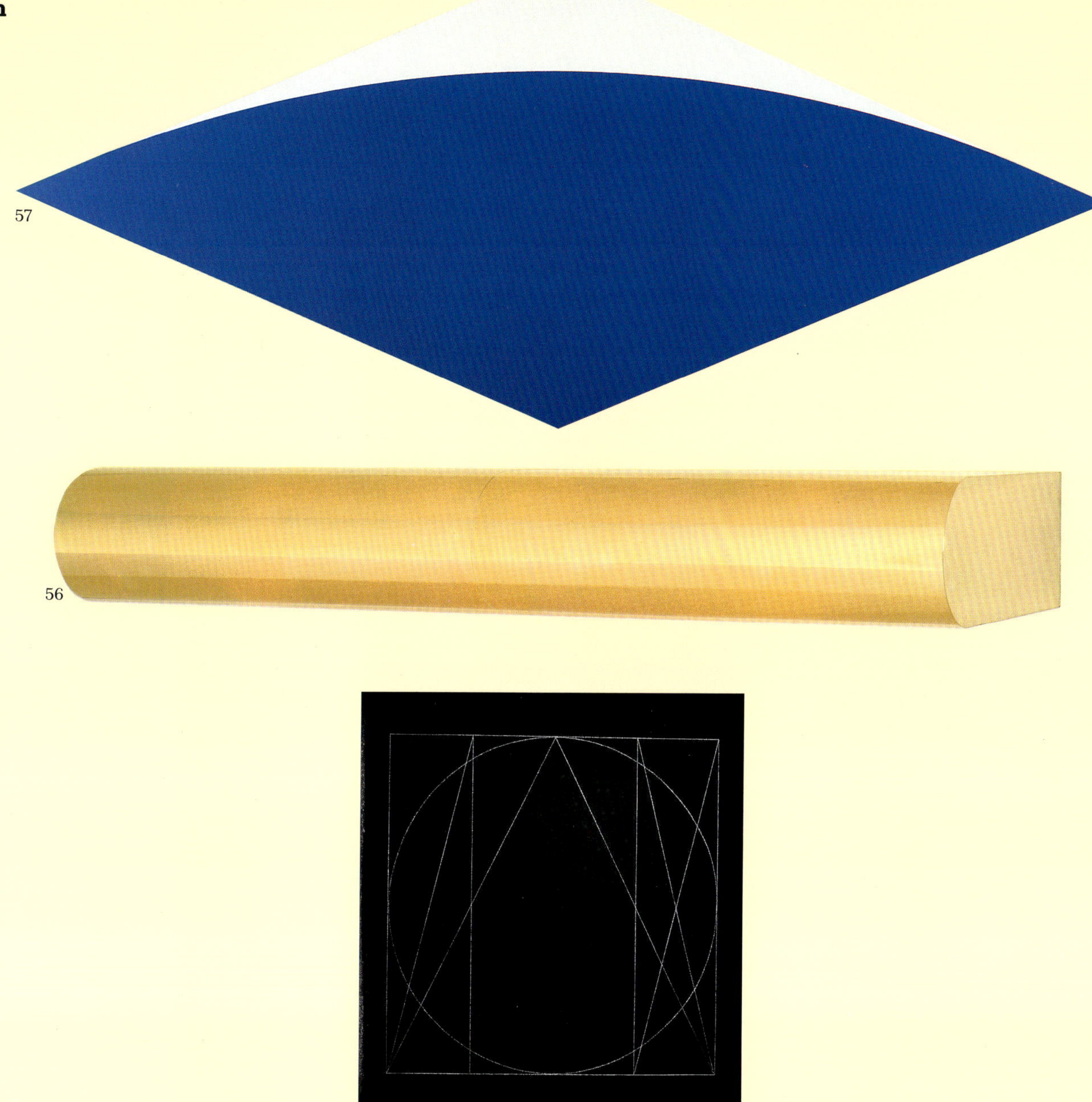

57

56

58

Minimalists concerned with simple geometric volumes—pyramids and cubes, for instance—emerged in America in the 1960s. Theirs was a profound reaction against the gestural art of the previous decade, in which the artistic process and artist's "handprint" were so essential. By contrast they sought to remove every indication of process, every trace of personality. The majority, Carl Andre and Donald Judd (no. 56) prominent among them, worked in sculpture with a smaller number, exemplified by Ellsworth Kelly (no. 57) and Sol LeWitt, working in painting. Some used readily available industrial materials or had their work fabricated by commercial foundries in order to distance themselves even further from the object-making aspect of art. LeWitt's drawings are conceptual works in which the artist issues a set of instructions for the execution of each piece that are to be followed each time it is re-created. In *Wall Drawing: Six Superimposed Geometric Figures*, 1976 (no. 58), the figures share a common center.

Frank Stella

60

61

59

Frank Stella was one of the first of the generation of artists to react against the spontaneous gesture and loose brushwork of Abstract Expressionism, proposing in its stead an art that stressed control and rationalism over freedom of expression. Attempting to deny any remnant of illusory space, he advocated a kind of painting based on the notion that "only what can be seen there is there." By extending wide bands of black enamel and stripes of unpainted canvas to the very edge of the picture, he defined his daring Black paintings (no. 59) as objects. The Aluminum series of the sixties intensified this control and austerity, creating a group of large, "shaped" architectonic canvases. His paintings came "off the wall" in the early seventies as he introduced relief and depth in his Polish Village series. Later in the decade he explored new possibilities in abstraction, challenging the distinctions between painting and sculpture. For paintings in the Exotic Bird series, like *Kagu*, 1979 – 80 (no. 60), he cut complicated reliefs from brashly colored metal, and in the Malta series *St. Michael's Counterguard*, 1984 (no. 61), Stella actually breaks through the picture plane in his continuing examination of the structure of painting, relying more on bold, interpenetrating shapes than on a varied palette.

Seventies Abstract Painting

62

64

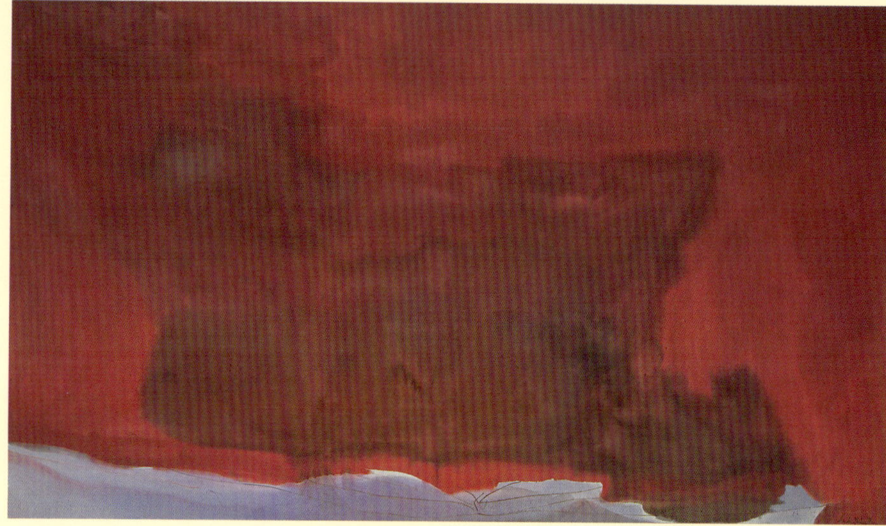
63

After a decade of figurative painting Diebenkorn returned to abstraction with his Ocean Park series, paintings based on his experience of light and dependent for their color and pictorial structure on the artist's deeply felt relationship with the art of the past, especially that of Matisse. Spacious and flat at the same time, the Ocean Park paintings are airy and full of light (no. 62). ■ Frankenthaler has continued painting the colorful abstractions begun in the fifties. In *Renaissance*, 1971 (no. 63), she is preoccupied with areas of modulated color on a large canvas and the ways in which "accidents" are controlled. Her lyrical approach to color is enhanced by thin washes that stain the raw canvas. ■ Throughout the seventies Ronald Davis created a series of large canvases (no. 64) on which immense geometric volumes intersect and perspective is a key issue.

The Eighties: New Expressions

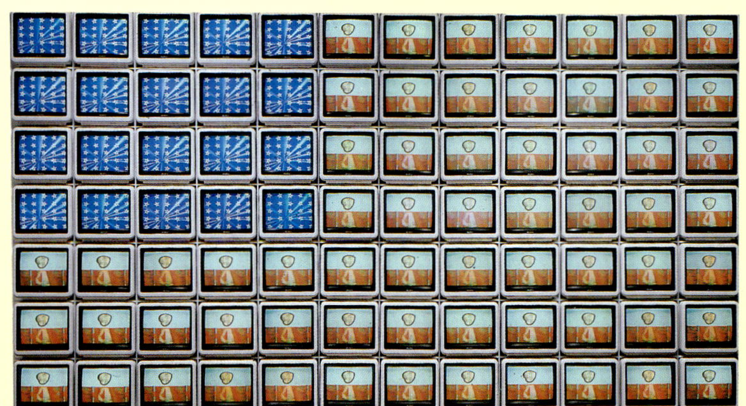
74

65

66

The seventies were a time when numerous artists professed an aversion to painting and object making, a time when concepts, language, and ideas were primary concerns. Artists who matured when the climate was inhospitable to content-laden art are returning with vigor in the eighties to painting and sculpture. Their painting and sculpture are newly imbued with narrative content, charged with social and political meaning, and invested with emotion. Many empathize with the energetic gesture of the Abstract Expressionists or the turbulent substance of German Expressionism. Not only in America but in Europe as well this spirit is flourishing. ■ David Hockney and Jim Dine (no. 65) continue their twenty-year explorations of representation with fresh insight. Hockney's ambitious *Mulholland Drive*, 1980 (no. 66), followed almost a decade's involvement with stage design and a renewed interest in Picasso's work occasioned by the 1980 Museum of Modern Art retrospective. Neil Jenney was among the first artists to be associated with the new spirit in painting and sculpture of the eighties. His *Acid Story*, 1983–84 (no. 67), reflects his concern with social issues in a large canvas evoking nineteenth-century American luminism in its exquisite surface quality. Susan Rothenberg's paintings of the mid-1970s were distinctive images of horses in profile in which she

75

73

communicated states of mind. In the early 1980s she created images like *Snowman*, 1983 (no. 68), that were less controlled, less distanced, and began to focus on the human figure. Anselm Kiefer, a German artist, tackles evocations of wartorn landscape and German history in eloquent paintings and in this rare sculpture, *The Book*, 1985 (no. 69), making recurrent use of evocative symbols—ladders, fires, wings—as well as texts that enrich his imagery. This monumental sculpture can be seen as a summation of many of his concerns. Bruce Nauman's messages pulsate in neon sculptures whose beauty belies their urgency (no. 70). Artists such as Jonathan Borofsky conflate the media—painting and sculpture—in complex, room-sized environments with large moving figures (no. 71). Beginning in the 1960s Robert Morris pioneered developments in conceptual art, minimal and environmental sculpture, earth, performance, and installation art. In the late 1970s he introduced depictive imagery; in *Order*, 1985 (no. 72), from his recent Burning Planet Series, he combines elements of painting and sculpture in a political and historical statement. Nam June Paik continues a two-decade involvement with video in his *Video Flag z,* 1986 (no. 74), a complex installation of eighty-four television sets.

The Eighties: New Expressions

70

71

67

69

68

72

1. **Pablo Picasso**
Born Spain, active in France, 1881–1973
Portrait of Sebastián Juñer Vidal, 1903
Oil on canvas
49¾ x 37 in.
Bequest of David E. Bright
M.67.25.18

2. **Maurice Vlaminck**
France, 1876–1958
Portrait of Apollinaire, 1903
Oil on board
21¼ x 17½ in.
Promised gift of Marion and Nathan Smooke

3. **Henri Matisse**
France, 1869–1954
Standing Male Nude, 1900
Oil on canvas
30 x 22 in.
Promised gift of Marion and Nathan Smooke

4. **Henri Matisse**
France, 1869–1954
Heads of Jeannette, 1910–13
Bronze
Height: each approx. 20 in.
Presented by the Art Museum Council in memory of Penelope Rigby
68.3.1–.2, M.68.48.1–.3

5. **Henri Matisse**
France, 1869–1954
Tea, 1919
Oil on canvas
55 x 83 in.
Bequest of David L. Loew in memory of his father, Marcus Loew
M.74.52.2

6. **Mikhail Larionov**
Russia, 1881–1954
Dancing Soldiers, 1909–10
Oil on canvas
34⅝ x 40⅛ in.
Purchased with funds provided by the Mr. and Mrs. William Preston Harrison Collection, Mr. and Mrs. John C. Best, Friends of the Museum, Charles Feldman, and Mr. and Mrs. Paul Kantor
80.3

7. **Marc Chagall**
Born Russia, active in France, 1887–1985
Violinist in the Snow, c. 1912
Oil on canvas
40 x 30 in.
Gift of Mrs. Mary Day McLane
64.6

8. **Georges Braque**
France, 1882–1963
Still Life with Violin, 1914
Oil on canvas
36½ x 26 in.
Purchased with funds provided by the Mr. and Mrs. George Gard De Sylva Collection and the Copley Foundation
M.86.128

9. **Alexander Archipenko**
Born Russia, active in the United States, 1887–1964
Woman with Hat, 1916
Wood, metal, papier mache, gauze, and paint
17⅝ x 14¼ in.
Purchased with funds provided by the Loula D. Lasker estate and Merle Oberon
M.86.130

10. **Fernand Léger**
France, 1881–1955
The Disks, 1918–19
Oil on canvas
51⅛ x 38¼ in.
Bequest of David E. Bright
M.67.25.2

11. **František Kupka**
Czechoslovakia, 1871–1957
Irregular Forms: Creation, 1911
Oil on canvas
42½ x 42½ in.
Bequest of David E. Bright
M.67.25.10

12. **Alexandr Rodchenko**
Russia, 1891–1956
Untitled, c. 1920
Oil on wood
33½ x 25¼ in.
Gift of Anna Bing Arnold
M.80.119

13. **El Lissitzky**
Russia, 1890–1941
Proun 3A, c. 1920
Oil on canvas
28 x 23 in.
Purchased with funds provided by Mr. and Mrs. David E. Bright and the bequest of David E. Bright
86.3

14. **Wassily Kandinsky**
Born Russia, active in Germany and France, 1866–1944
Sign, 1925
Oil on cardboard
27⅛ x 19¼ in.
Museum acquisition by exchange from David E. Bright bequest
M.86.101

15. **Piet Mondrian**
Holland, 1872–1944
Composition in White, Red and Yellow, 1938
Oil on canvas
31½ x 24½ in.
Mr. and Mrs. William Preston Harrison Collection
63.14

16. **Kurt Schwitters**
Germany, 1887–1948
Construction for Noble Ladies, 1919
Cardboard, wood, metal, and paint
40½ x 33 in.
Purchased with funds provided by Mr. and Mrs. Norton Simon, the Junior Arts Council, Mr. and Mrs. Frederick R. Weisman, Mr. and Mrs. Taft Schreiber, Mr. Hans de Schulthess, Mr. and Mrs. Edwin Janss, and Mr. and Mrs. Gifford Phillips
M.62.22

17. **Karl Schmidt-Rottluff**
Germany, 1884–1976
Bathers, 1913
Oil on canvas
34½ x 39¼ in.
Gift of Josef von Sternberg
46.26.3

18. **Ernst Ludwig Kirchner**
Germany, 1880–1938
Two Women, 1911/22
Oil on canvas
59 x 47 in.
Gift of B. Gerald Cantor
60.33

19. **Wassily Kandinsky**
Born Russia, active in Germany and France, 1866–1944
Untitled Improvisation III, 1914
Oil on cardboard
25⅝ x 19¾ in.
Museum acquistion by exchange from David E. Bright bequest
M.85.151

20. **Ludwig Meidner**
Germany, 1884–1966
Apocalyptic Landscape, 1914
Oil on canvas
37½ x 31⅝ in.
Gift of Clifford Odets
60.65.1

21. **Otto Dix**
Germany, 1891–1969
Leda, 1919
Oil on canvas
40¾ x 31¾ in.
Purchased with funds provided by Charles K. Feldman, Mr. and Mrs. John C. Best, and B. Gerald Cantor
85.3

22. **Ernst Barlach**
Germany, 1870–1938
The Beggar, 1930/cast 1984
Bronze 3/8
85⅜ x 22⅞ x 17¾ in.
Gift of Anna Bing Arnold
M.84.97

23. **Hermann Scherer**
Switzerland, 1893–1927
Sleeping Woman with Boy, 1926
Painted wood
19½ x 53¼ x 21½ in.
Gift of Anna Bing Arnold
M.84.30

24. **Albert Müller**
Switzerland, 1897–1926
Standing Figure, 1924
Wood
h.: 41⅜ in.
Purchased with funds provided by Alexander M. Lewyt
84.3

25. **René Magritte**
Belgium, 1898–1967
The Treachery of Images (Ceci n'est pas une pipe,) c. 1928–29
Oil on canvas
25⅜ x 37 in.
Purchased with funds provided by the Mr. and Mrs. William Preston Harrison Collection
78.7

26. **Pablo Picasso**
Born Spain, active in France, 1881–1973
Centaur, 1955
Painted wood
90 x 79 x 29 in.
Partial gift of Gloria and David L. Wolper
M.85.318

27. **Marcel Duchamp**
France, active in the United States, 1887–1968
From or by Marcel Duchamp or Rrose Sélavy [The Box in a Valise], 1955–68
Leather-covered case containing miniature replicas and color reproductions of works by Duchamp
16⅛ x 14⅞ x 4⅛ in.
Promised gift of the Grinstein family

28. **Man Ray**
United States, active in France, 1890–1976
Cadeau (Gift), 1963 replica of 1921 original
Flat iron with nails
5½ x 3½ x 3½ in.
Promised gift of the Michael and Dorothy Blankfort Collection

29. **Alberto Giacometti**
Switzerland, 1901–66
Large Standing Woman IV, 1966
Bronze
106 x 13⅛ x 22 in.
Gift of Mr. and Mrs. David L. Wolper
M.83.204.2

30. **Joan Miró**
Spain, 1893–1983
Animated Forms, 1935
Oil on canvas
75½ x 68 in.
Bequest of David E. Bright
M.67.25.3

31. **Arshile Gorky**
Born Armenia, active in the United States, 1904–48
Mojave, 1941–42
Oil on canvas
28¾ x 40½ in.
Gift of Burt Kleiner
M.64.61

32. **Jackson Pollock**
United States, 1912–56
Black and White Number 20, 1951
Duco on canvas
57⅛ x 64 in.
Bequest of David E. Bright
M.67.25.16

33. **Jean Dubuffet**
France, 1901–85
The Effacement of Memories, 1957
Oil on canvas
35 x 46 in.
Bequest of David E. Bright
M.67.25.15

34. **Franz Kline**
United States, 1910–62
The Ballantine, 1948–60
Oil on canvas
72 x 72 in.
Bequest of David E. Bright
M.67.25.20

35. **Willem de Kooning**
Born Holland 1904, active in the United States
Montauk Highway, 1958
Oil on canvas
59 x 48 in.
Promised gift of the Michael and Dorothy Blankfort Collection

36. **Richard Diebenkorn**
United States, born 1922
Freeway and Aqueduct, 1957
Oil on canvas
23¼ x 28 in.
Partial gift of William and Regina Fadiman
M.86.68

37. **Helen Frankenthaler**
United States, born 1928
Winter Hunt, 1958
Oil on canvas
91 x 46½ in.
Gift of David Geffen
M.85.157

38. **Morris Louis**
United States, 1912–62
Beta Ro from the Unfurled Series, 1959–60
Acrylic on canvas
103 x 161 in.
Gift of Mr. and Mrs. Frederick R. Weisman
M.77.164

39. **Mark Rothko**
Born Latvia, active in the United States, 1903–70
White Center, 1957
Oil on canvas
84 x 72 in.
Bequest of David E. Bright
M.67.25.21

40. **Sam Francis**
United States, born 1923
Toward Disappearance, 1957
Oil on canvas
108 x 144 in.
Modern and Contemporary Art Council Fund
M.70.14

41. **Isamu Noguchi**
United States, born 1904
Cronos, 1947/cast 1986
Bronze
h.: 87 in.
Purchased with funds provided by James and Ilene Nathan and promised gift of James and Ilene Nathan and Nate and Sandy Seltzer.
M.86.146

42. **David Smith**
United States, 1906–65
Cubi XXIII, 1964
Stainless steel
76¼ x 172⅞ in.
Modern and Contemporary Art Council Fund
M.67.26

43. **Lucas Samaras**
Born Greece 1936, active in the United States
Untitled, 1963
Box, photographs, pins, and colored yarn
10¼ x 14⅜ x 8 in.
Promised gift of the Michael and Dorothy Blankfort Collection

44. **H. C. Westermann**
United States, 1922–81
Tension, 1967
Wood and metal
21 x 28 x 9¼ in.
The Harry Lenart Fund
M.85.61

45. **Edward Kienholz**
United States, born 1927
A Lady Named Zoe, 1960
Paint, fiberglass, mannequin parts, dispensing machine, enameling kiln, and stool
64 x 18 x 18 in.
Partial gift of Mrs. Lillian Alpers

46. **Edward Kienholz**
United States, born 1927
The Back Seat Dodge '38, 1964
Paint, 1938 Dodge, chicken wire, flocking, beer bottles, artificial grass, and cast plaster
66 x 240 x 144 in.
Purchased with funds provided by the Art Museum Council
M.81.248a–e

47. **Claes Oldenburg**
Born Sweden 1929, active in the United States
Giant Pool Balls, 1967
balls: Plexiglas
diam.: each ball 24 in.
rack: metal
20 x 120 x 108 in.
Anonymous gift through the Contemporary Art Council
M.69.88

48. **Roy Lichtenstein**
United States, born 1923
Cold Shoulder, 1963
Magna on canvas
68 x 48 in.
Promised gift of Robert H. Halff

49. **Andy Warhol**
United States, born 1930
Black and White Disaster, 1962
Acrylic and silkscreen enamel on canvas
96 x 72 in.
Gift of Leo Castelli Gallery and Ferus Gallery through the Contemporary Art Council
M.65.13

50. **George Segal**
United States, born 1924
Old Woman at a Window, 1965
Plaster, painted wood, glass, chrome, and board
96 x 36 x 48 in.
Gift of Pauli and Mel Hirsh
M.83.209a–d

51. **Ed Ruscha**
United States, born 1937
Actual Size, 1962
Oil on canvas
72 x 67 in.
Anonymous gift through the Contemporary Art Council
M.63.14

52. **John Mason**
United States, born 1927
Red X, 1966
Ceramic
58½ x 59½ x 17 in.
Gift of the Burt Kleiner Foundation
M.73.38.11

53. **Kenneth Price**
United States, born 1935
Unit 3 from Happy's Curios, 1972–77
Ceramic with wood cabinet
cabinet: 70 x 21 x 21¼ in.
Gift of Betty M. Asher
M.83.229.25a–r

54. **Robert Arneson**
United States, born 1930
Way West of Athens, 1983
Bronze on ceramic base
72¾ x 21¼ x 21¼ in.
The Harry Lenart Fund
M.85.63a–b

55. **Dale Chihuly**
United States, born 1941
Seaform, 1981
Free-blown and expanded mold-blown and tooled glass
9 x 19½ in.
Gift of Daniel and Susan Greenberg
M.84.201.1a–e

56. **Donald Judd**
United States, born 1928
Bullnose, 1974
Brass
10⅛ x 72 x 26⅛ in.
Purchased with matching funds provided by the National Endowment for the Arts and the Modern and Contemporary Art Council
M.74.129

57. **Ellsworth Kelly**
United States, born 1923
Blue Curve III, 1972
Oil on canvas
67¾ x 166½ in.
Purchased with funds provided by Paul Rosenberg & Company, Mrs. Lita A. Hazen, and the bequest of David E. Bright
M.73.7

58. **Sol LeWitt**
United States, born 1928
Wall Drawing: Six Superimposed Geometric Figures, 1976
White chalk on black wall
120 x 132 in.
Purchased with matching funds provided by the National Endowment for the Arts and the Modern and Contemporary Art Council
M.76.103

59. **Frank Stella**
United States, born 1936
Getty Tomb, 1959
Enamel on canvas
84 x 96 in.
Purchased with funds provided by the Contemporary Art Council
M.63.21

60. **Frank Stella**
United States, born 1936
Kagu from the Exotic Bird series, 1979–80
Mixed media on aluminum
93 x 110 in.
Purchased with funds provided by Phil and Bea Gersh, the Modern and Contemporary Art Council Fund, and a matching grant from the National Endowment for the Arts
M.80.137

61. **Frank Stella**
United States, born 1936
St. Michael's Counterguard from the Malta series, 1984
Mixed media on aluminum and fiberglass honeycomb
156 x 135 x 108 in.
Gift of Anna Bing Arnold
M.84.150

62. **Richard Diebenkorn**
United States, born 1922
Ocean Park Series No. 49, 1972
Oil on canvas
93 x 81 in.
Purchased with funds provided by Paul Rosenberg & Company, Mrs. Lita A. Hazen, and the bequest of David E. Bright
M.73.96

63. **Helen Frankenthaler**
United States, born 1928
Renaissance, 1971
Acrylic on canvas
92½ x 163 in.
Purchased with funds provided by the Art Museum Council
M.81.95

64. **Ronald Davis**
United States, born 1937
Splatter Galaxy, 1982
Acrylic on canvas
114 x 184¾ in.
Promised gift of Sue and Steven Antebi

65. **Jim Dine**
United States, born 1935
Study for the Sculpture of Crommelynck Gate with Tools (Hobby Horse), 1983
Mixed media on paper with objects
69 x 91 in.
Gift of Alan Shayne
M.85.317

66. **David Hockney**
Born England 1937, active in the United States
Mulholland Drive: The Road to the Studio, 1980
Acrylic on canvas
86 x 243 in.
Purchased with funds provided by the F. Patrick Burns bequest
M.83.35
©David Hockney 1980

67. **Neil Jenney**
United States, born 1945
Acid Story, 1983–84
Oil on wood
34½ x 140 x 5 in.
Promised gift of Steve Martin

68. **Susan Rothenberg**
United States, born 1945
Snowman, 1983
Oil on canvas
79 x 86½ x 1⅝ in.
Purchased with funds provided by Ray Stark
M.84.11

69. **Anselm Kiefer**
Germany, born 1945
The Book, 1985
Lead, steel, and tin
114 x 213½ x 34 in.
Modern and Contemporary Art Council Fund and Louise and Harold Held
M.85.376

70. **Bruce Nauman**
United States, born 1941
Human Nature/Life Death/Knows Doesn't Know, 1983
Neon and glass tubing
107½ x 107 x 5¾ in.
Purchased with funds provided by the Modern and Contemporary Art Council
M.84.36

71. **Jonathan Borofsky**
United States, born 1942
Hammering Man, 1983
Painted wood and electric motor
h.: 180 in.
Purchased with funds provided by the Modern and Contemporary Art Council and Bea and Phil Gersh
M.83.167

72. **Robert Morris**
United States, born 1931
Order from the Burning Planet Series, 1985
Painted cast hydrocal, oil on canvas, and fiberglass
112 x 147 x 24 in.
Purchased with funds provided by the Collectors Committee
M.86.129

73. **Peter Alexander**
United States, born 1939
Gulper, 1981
Collage on velvet
73¾ x 88 in.
Purchased with funds provided by the Modern and Contemporary Art Council
M.81.246

74. **Nam June Paik**
Born Korea 1932, active in the United States
Video Flag z, 1986
Color television sets, videocassette players, videotapes, and Plexiglas modular cabinet
74½ x 138¾ x 18 in.
Gift of the Art Museum Council

75. **Nancy Graves**
United States, born 1940
Trace, 1981
Painted Corten steel and aluminum
192 x 214 x 120 in.
Gift of Joseph Haddad in memory of Jaye Haddad
M.85.315

Supervisors and Trustees